RESCUE

The Story of How Gentiles
Saved Jews in the Holocaust

Also by Milton Meltzer

NEVER TO FORGET
The Jews of the Holocaust

AIN'T GONNA STUDY WAR NO MORE
The Story of America's Peace Seekers

THE BLACK AMERICANS
A History in Their Own Words, 1619–1983

THE AMERICAN REVOLUTIONARIES
A History in Their Own Words, 1750–1800

THE JEWISH AMERICANS
A History in Their Own Words

THE HISPANIC AMERICANS

THE CHINESE AMERICANS

ALL TIMES, ALL PEOPLES
A World History of Slavery

THE TERRORISTS

THE LANDSCAPE OF MEMORY

POVERTY IN AMERICA

LANGSTON HUGHES
A Biography

MARK TWAIN
A Writer's Life

GEORGE WASHINGTON
AND THE BIRTH OF OUR NATION

WINNIE MANDELA
The Soul of South Africa

RESCUE

The Story of How Gentiles Saved Jews in the Holocaust

by **Milton Meltzer**

HARPER & ROW, PUBLISHERS
Cambridge, Philadelphia, San Francisco,
St. Louis, London, Singapore, Sydney
NEW YORK

In memory of my grandparents—
Samuel and Rose Richter,
and Michael and Leah Meltzer

Rescue: The Story of How Gentiles Saved Jews in the Holocaust
Copyright © 1988 by Milton Meltzer
All rights reserved. No part of this book may be
used or reproduced in any manner whatsoever without
written permission except in the case of brief quotations
embodied in critical articles and reviews. Printed in
the United States of America. For information address
Harper & Row Junior Books, 10 East 53rd Street,
New York, N.Y. 10022. Published simultaneously in
Canada by Fitzhenry & Whiteside Limited, Toronto.
Printed in the U.S.A. All rights reserved.
Typography by Pat Tobin
10 9 8 7 6 5 4 3 2 1
First Edition

Library of Congress Cataloging-in-Publication Data
Meltzer, Milton, date
    Rescue
    Bibliography: p.
    Includes index.
    Summary: A recounting drawn from historic source
material of the many individual acts of heroism
performed by righteous gentiles who sought to thwart the
extermination of the Jews during the Holocaust.
    1. World War, 1939–1945—Jews—Rescue—Juvenile
literature.   2. Righteous Gentiles in the Holocaust—
Juvenile literature.   3. Holocaust, Jewish (1939–1945)—
Juvenile literature.   [1. World War, 1939–1945—Jews—
Rescue.   2. Holocaust, Jewish (1939–1945)]   I. Title.
D810.J4M3893 1988   940.53'15'03924   87-47816
ISBN 0-06-024209-4
ISBN 0-06-024210-8 (lib. bdg.)

CONTENTS

FINLAND
Helsinki

EUROPE UNDER
NAZI OCCUPATION

Tallinn
Leningrad
ESTONIA

LATVIA
Riga

Moscow

LITHUANIA
Kovno
Vilna

Tula

EAST
PRUSSIA

Minsk

SOVIET UNION

POLAND
UNDER
GERMAN
RULE

Warsaw
łz

Plaszow
Cracow
Tarnopol
Auschwitz Lvov

Kharkov

Stalingrad

Kiev

Rostov

UKRAINE

TRANSNISTRIA

VAKIA

Budapest

NGARY

CRIMEA

RUMANIA
Bucharest

Black Sea

Belgrade
SERBIA

Sofia

BULGARIA

ALBANIA

Istanbul

Ankara

GREECE

TURKEY

Athens

Crete

Cyprus

Sea

The first question that the Levite asked was, "If I stop to help this man, what will happen to me?" But then the good Samaritan came by. And he reversed the question. "If I do not stop to help this man, what will happen to him?" That is the question before you.

—FROM THE LAST SPEECH OF MARTIN LUTHER KING, JR., MEMPHIS, TENNESSEE, APRIL 1968

1 A Darkness Everywhere

This is a book about the Gentile men and women, and children too, who had the courage to risk their lives and those of their families in the rescue of Jews during the Nazi era. Some thousands of Jewish lives were saved. Against six million lost in the Holocaust, how many is that? Yet few as the rescuers were, they must not be forgotten.

Their stories let us know that while there were victims, there were also heroes and heroines. What they did makes us see that we need not give in to evil. There are other choices than passive acceptance, or complicity. There are human spirits who resist. They are witness to the goodness in humanity.

More than ten years ago I wrote *Never to Forget: The Jews of the Holocaust,* a book that told in considerable detail how and when the Holocaust happened. In that book I used eyewitness accounts, diaries, journals, memoirs, interviews of those who experienced the terror and the grief of that era. I concentrated on the history of hatred that led up to the catastrophe, on the processes of destruction, and finally on the Jews' spirit of resistance. The focus was on the central issue of what part of the world did and all of the world permitted to be done. But I said almost nothing about the people some call the "Righteous Gentiles"—the non-Jews in Germany and every country of Nazi-occupied Europe who helped many of Adolf Hitler's victims.

Now I have come to realize the great importance of recording not just the evidence of evil, but also the evidence of human nobility. Love, not hatred, is what the world needs. Rescue, not destruction. The stories in this book offer reason to hope. And hope is what we need, the way plants need sunlight.

Here I will briefly give the general background to the story of the rescuers of Jews. The following chapters will be more specific on the causes of events in the countries or regions I describe.

"The Holocaust" is the term Jews themselves chose to describe what happened to them during World War II. The term is related to the word *olah* in the Hebrew Bible. Its religious meaning is "burnt sacrifice." Over the 3500-year span of Jewish history, the Holocaust was the most massive catastrophe. Six million died, two out of every three Jews in Europe, one third of the world's Jews. But don't think of them as "millions." Do that and you miss the truth of the murder of each *individual* man, woman, and child.

The German code name for the systematic murder of the Jews was the "Final Solution of the Jewish Problem." It was Hitler's prime goal, set forth in his book *Mein Kampf* (My Struggle), a book that almost nobody took seriously when it was first published in 1925. He carried out his goal with iron will and mechanical efficiency, even when it interfered with his war against the Allied nations.

Persecution, torment, murder were not new to the Jews. They had suffered them for millennia. So had other peoples. They were massacred for what chiefs, kings, emperors, dictators called useful goals. The victims died because those in power wanted to increase that power, to grab wealth or territory, to crush opposition, to force conversion. The powerful persecuted the weak whenever they believed it to be in their own interest.

It was different with Hitler and the Nazis. They wanted to kill all Jews solely because they were Jews. Their crime? They were accused of living, of having been born. Such a crime had no precedent. The murder of Jews had nothing to do with their faith, or lack of faith. Hitler hated them because of what he called their "race." The Nazis said the Jews were "inferior" and therefore had no right to live in the same world with their "superiors," the Germans.

Jews are people like any other—good, bad, gifted, stupid, cheerful, sad, weak, strong, greedy, generous. But to Hitler that didn't matter. All that mattered was that they were Jews. And his policy demanded their total annihilation as a people.

The mass murder that followed was a crime against all humanity. That the Jews were the victims was the outcome of a long history of anti-Semitism in Germany, in Europe, in the world. But what Hitler did was to make the possibility of suffering a Holocaust a reality for any group of people. As a result, ever since the Holocaust no group has been able to feel it can never know the same fate.

To put the story in perspective requires a look back in

history for the roots of anti-Semitism. Its religious base lies in the Christian Gospels: the accusation that the Jews were to blame for the crucifixion of Jesus. When "Christ-killer" became a synonym for Jew, persecution inevitably followed. For many centuries both church and state took steps to punish Jews and to ensure their misery. Decrees kept them from farming the land or practicing the crafts. The Crusades that began in 1096 marked the beginning of an oppression the duration and intensity of which would not be equaled until Hitler's time. The Crusaders who set off to free the Holy Land from the Moslem infidels began by killing the Jewish infidels they encountered passing through Europe. Christians massacred Jews on a stunning scale. From 1215 on, the church forced Jews to wear a distinctive badge on their clothing. They were blamed for anything that went wrong. But when money made from the occupations they were restricted to—trade and banking—could be sluiced into the treasuries of kings and nobles, they were tolerated. When that usefulness was gone, they were expelled. They were forced to live behind ghetto walls. Some migrated to the New World or settled in Eastern Europe.

In the sixteenth century, when Martin Luther founded his new faith, he championed the Jews. But when he failed to win them to Protestantism, he revived all the old charges. Jews were called ritual murderers, usurers, poisoners, parasites, devils. He urged the burning of their synagogues, the seizure of their books, and their expulsion from Germany.

As the Industrial Revolution developed in Western Europe, new ideas about the rights of man emerged. The movement for Enlightenment promised civil rights for

4

the Jews. Young middle-class Jews wanted to break free of the ghetto; they answered eagerly to the call for liberty, equality, fraternity. They devoted themselves to modern education and began to make their mark on Western culture. After the French Revolution of 1789 Napoleon's armies carried the banner of freedom into other countries, and Jews became citizens with full rights. But only briefly, in many places.

In Germany, the defeat of Napoleon and the rise of nationalism made Jews outsiders again. Their political rights were reduced or taken away completely. Germans created a "science" of anti-Semitism, based on racial identity. It held that Jews were born a "slave race," while the Germans or Aryans were the "master race." Nature, it was held, had created all Jews physically and morally inferior.

A stream of anti-Semitic books and pamphlets polluted German culture. "Good" Jews? "Bad" Jews? What difference did it make? All Jews were considered the same. Even the baptized and assimilated Jew was worthless to the anti-Semite. For it was no longer a question of religion. The Jews' "race," their "blood," condemned them.

This vicious nonsense became powerful political propaganda. By the time Adolf Hitler was born in 1889, anti-Semitic political parties were polling hundreds of thousands of votes and electing many deputies to the German Reichstag. "The Jews Are Our Misfortune" was a slogan blazoned on banners and spread in print. One prominent German philosopher, Karl Eugen Dühring, wrote that the Jews are "inferior and depraved. . . . The duty of the Nordic peoples is to exterminate such parasitic races as we exterminate snakes and beasts of prey."

That deadly conviction became an article of German faith. When Hitler built his Nazi party in the 1920s, he used anti-Semitism brilliantly, if insanely, to cement together workers and industrialists, land barons and peasants, fools and intellectuals, atheists and preachers, young and old. It was the magic formula to solve all of Germany's social problems. He made it a weapon against all opposition. The Jew was no longer merely a scapegoat. He was the cause of every problem, the essence of all evil. And nothing could redeem the Jew. He was born subhuman. The only solution to this "Jewish problem," said Hitler, was to destroy them all. They had no right to live.

Hitler won power in January 1933. In the next several years he solidified his dictatorship over Germany and sowed the seeds of the Holocaust. He abolished all political parties but his own, wiped out the labor unions, and jailed their leaders. He eliminated unemployment by a program of vast public works and rearmament and by drafting youth into the armed forces. He took total control of all the media and the financial institutions. A poisonous mixture of Nazi schooling, youth organizations, and propaganda convinced the young they were a race of "true" Germans. "It is my duty," Hitler said, "to make use of every means of training the German people to cruelty, and to prepare them for war. . . . A violently active, dominating, intrepid, brutal youth—that is what I am after. Youth must be all this. It must be indifferent to pain. There must be no weakness or tenderness in it."

Hitler made sure that the top command of the army would follow his orders. His Gestapo agents (the secret police) spied on the public's everyday behavior, monitored party and government functions, ran concentration camps, and later carried out mass killings. His black-shirted security police, the SS, led by Heinrich Himmler, shaped an elite of Nazi fanatics into another major instrument of terror. Concentration camps were built to confine anyone suspected of active or potential opposition.

With full control of power, Hitler began step by step to isolate and terrorize the Jews. How many were there in the Germany of 1933? Only half a million, less than 1 percent of the population. No matter how few, the Nazis daily repeated the lie that the Jews had dominated industry, finance, government, and that this must end.

The Jews were expelled from the civil service, the army, the schools, the professions. The Nuremberg Laws of 1935 and the decrees that followed took away their citizenship and restricted their housing, their shopping, their schooling, their every movement. Violence against the Jews grew. When beatings and killings made the foreign press, the Nazis watched for public and governmental reaction. When little of consequence happened, the Nazis knew they could attack Jews with impunity.

Growing ever bolder, in 1936 Hitler violated the Versailles Treaty that ended World War I by placing troops in the Rhineland region; no one tried to stop him. That summer he played host to the Olympic Games in Berlin; no countries refused to participate. In March 1938 he sent troops into Austria and made the country part of "Greater Germany"; no one interfered. In September of that year he played on popular fear in England and France of another war and got their government leaders to sign a pact at Munich that put Czechoslovakia in his hands. The West gave thanks in the false hope that "peace in our time" was guaranteed.

And the Jews in Germany? Stripped of citizenship, rights,

work, property, dignity, they had only one way out: emigration. By late 1937 about 130,000 had fled. But three quarters of Germany's Jews still remained. Hitler tried to dump them across his borders, but "almost every state in the world has hermetically sealed its borders against the parasitical Jewish intruder," complained the German Foreign Office. It was true. The non-Nazi countries of Europe and the United States took in some Jewish refugees, but pitifully few in relation to the desperate need. Even so, some German Jews still hoped they would survive somehow, that a decent, democratic, moral government would replace Hitler's and make Germany once again their safe home.

In 1938 that illusion was smashed. The assassination of a minor officer in the German embassy in Paris by a refugee Jew triggered a nationwide pogrom in Germany on the night of November 9. The *Kristallnacht* (Night of Broken Glass) foreshadowed the extermination of the Jews. Most of Germany's synagogues were burned, thousands of shops destroyed, hundreds of homes looted. At least 1,000 Jews were murdered and 26,000 flung into concentration camps. That horror drove another 50,000 Jews out of Germany.

A year later it was too late to leave: The war Hitler started in the fall of 1939 cut off all exits. And at the same time Hitler invaded Poland, he pushed his war against the Jews to another stage. In a speech given shortly before the invasion Hitler had promised "the destruction of the Jewish race in Europe" when war began. With Poland quickly defeated, the Germans took complete control of millions of that country's Jews. Six months later Hitler conquered Denmark and Norway. Then Holland, Belgium, and France fell to the German armies. Only Britain was left in the West. Moving again toward the east, Hitler broke his pact with Stalin and invaded Russia in June 1941. His armies swiftly overran vast regions of the Soviet Union.

Under the cover of war he launched the murder of civilians. As soon as invasion of Poland began, mobile killing squads of the SS moved in with the German army and massacred captured Jews. The Jews were taken completely by surprise. No one could imagine such systematic murder of people without any reason whatever. Often the SS were helped by eager collaborators from the local population. By the end of the summer of 1942 one to two million Jews had been assassinated. (Exact counts were impossible.)

That was extermination by the bullet, Hitler's first method. The second method was starvation. Early in the war the Nazis decided to concentrate the Jews of Germany and the occupied countries in a small area. The interior of Poland was chosen. That region had several cities with very large numbers of Jews. Warsaw alone held half a million, the largest Jewish population of any city in the world except New York. All Jews living outside those Polish centers were herded by train, by truck, or on foot into closed-in ghettos set up in the cities.

Lublin, for instance, became the concentration point for Jews from western Poland, Bohemia (part of Czechoslovakia), and Austria. Before the war Lublin was the home of 40,000 Jews. Now, many times that number were penned into its ghetto. The journalist S. Moldawer described what he saw on the streets:

Lublin is a vale of sorrow. No human beings are they who walk its streets; all are phantoms, shadows, haunting a world that is no longer in evidence. Nobody speaks in Lublin; nobody exchanges greetings. They have even ceased to weep. . . . The congestion, the stench, the poverty, the disease and the chaos which reign in Lublin cannot be paralleled anywhere on earth. Men live in the streets, in cattle stalls, in cellars, in carts and in the debris of devastated houses.

Men die like flies in the thoroughfares, their bodies strewn on the roadway like old cinders. Shrouds are no longer used for the dead because none can be bought. . . . The whole city is girt with barbed wire fences, and the Nazis allow no traffic to pass through it. The water has turned foul and cannot be drunk. All the wells have become polluted. Cholera and typhus were already rampant when we reached Lublin. . . . The communal kitchen can actually serve nothing but potato broth and stale, black bread. Hundreds have not slept for weeks, cramped and confined in noisy freight cars. They wander about sad-eyed and distraught, like mourners at funerals. . . . One thing is clear as the day: the devil himself could not have devised such hell.

Many of the Jews in Lublin and the other ghettos were starved to death. That was cheaper than shooting them. The food grown in the occupied countries was taken by the Nazis and sent to Germany.

The "useful" ghetto Jews—those still able to work—were put to forced labor to clear away the rubble of war. Or, as large-scale projects began, the Nazis set up special concentration camps as slave-labor installations. The inmates dug canals and ditches, built roads and railways, reclaimed land. Factories were built near the camps, or camps near factories. Jewish slave labor was used to make airplanes, steel, munitions, military clothing—anything the Germans needed. But by the middle of 1944 the Jewish labor force was almost totally destroyed—by overwork, starvation, shooting. Valuable as their work was for military needs, Hitler's primary goal was their extermination.

The "unproductive" Jews—the weak, the sick, the old—were shot or forced to die from starvation and disease. But bullets were costly and hunger took its victims too slowly. Hitler couldn't wait that long. So gas was used. Jews were packed into buses with sealed windows and carbon monoxide from the exhausts was piped back into the buses. The buses were driven to pits, the doors opened, and the corpses shoveled out.

Adolf Eichmann—once a traveling salesman for an oil company, now a Nazi bureaucrat concerned with "Jewish affairs"—watched the gassing at Lodz. "Too slow," he said. So within a few months German technical ingenuity developed a way to speed up the killing process. A product called Zyklon B. (hydrogen cyanide) was made into bluish pellets, packed into small canisters, and poured through openings in the ceilings of the newly designed killing chambers. The Zyklon pellets turned into gas. It worked "fast"; within three to fifteen minutes, depending upon climatic conditions, everyone in the chamber would be dead. Hitler's experts had found the most efficient way of ridding the world of Jews.

But how to dispose of the bodies? At first bodies had been buried in mass graves. But the odor of decaying corpses spread for miles. And as the rate of killing mounted, the space needed for graves was enormous. (Furthermore, mass

11

graves were evidence of mass killings.) So cremation became the answer. Giant crematoriums were built. But by 1944, when over 10,000 Jews were being gassed every day, the ovens couldn't process that many bodies. So a cheaper and more efficient method was devised: burning corpses in open pits. It made a new record in destruction possible. In Auschwitz, by use of round-the-clock shifts, 34,000 people were killed every twenty-four hours.

"In those times," wrote Elie Wiesel, "there was darkness everywhere. In heaven and on earth, all the gates of compassion seemed to have been closed. The killer killed and the Jews died and the outside world adopted an attitude either of complicity or of indifference. Only a few had the courage to care."

2 The Countess Marushka

There were some who cared about what was happening to the Jews, and had the courage to act, even in Germany, the seat of Nazi power. Here was where the plans for mass murder were made, where Hitler took steps day by day, month by month, year by year, against the Jews. To understand how it could happen, it's necessary to realize that only *we* know how it ended. We know that it ended in mass murder. People living in Germany, at that time, did *not* know what the outcome would be. For both Jews and Christians the stages of destruction were totally new. The reality shocked them, paralyzed their minds. "Is what we see happening *really* happening?" It was unbelievable because there had never been anything like it before. So what Jews did in that terrible time, and what the Christians did, or failed to do, must be seen in that perspective.

Let's narrow the focus to Berlin, Hitler's capital. About 160,000 Jews lived in Berlin in 1933, the year the Nazis took control. Nearly seven years later, on the eve of World War II, about half that number remained. The others had migrated abroad, or disappeared, or killed themselves, or been murdered. The Jews were being eliminated during those seven years, but slowly.

As the killing centers in Poland were prepared, the Germans began deporting the Jews. Of course the Germans pretended they were simply "resettling" the Jews in the East. The German Jews were among the first of occupied Europe to be shipped east, for the Nazis were eager to rid their own country of the last Jew.

By the spring of 1942 there were still about 40,000 Jews left in Berlin. A year later more deportations and suicides had cut the number to 4,000. Joseph Goebbels, Hitler's propaganda chief and the political boss of Berlin, was enraged that even so few still survived. "Our plans were tipped off prematurely," he complained in his diary, "so that a lot of Jews slipped through our hands. They are now wandering about Berlin without homes, are not registered with police and are naturally quite a public danger." He ordered that everything possible be done "to round up these Jews."

Where were they? How had they managed to stay underground so long? Some had hidden successfully on their own, without help from anyone. But others were still alive by the grace of Gentiles.

What kinds of help could Gentiles give beleaguered Jews? They could hide them in their home. Provide false documents to conceal identity. Supply food. Help smuggle Jews out of the country.

To hide a Jew required courage, for you risked your own family's life. But it required even more than courage. You had to find the right place to hide someone and be able to conceal it. You also knew that often survival demanded frequent changes in hiding places. If you hid a number of Jews in a private home, whether in town or in the country, it could easily end in exposure by suspicious neighbors. And what about feeding people in hiding? In a city you might be able to buy small amounts of extra food in scattered black markets. But it was much harder to do in smaller places. And if the hideaway didn't have inside toilets (and many did not), how did you dispose of wastes? What could you do if a pregnant woman was about to give birth? How did you get a doctor for a sick Jew? How did you bury one who died in hiding? What if little children cried when an unknowing neighbor dropped in or the SS came to snoop?

Necessity made Gentiles brilliant at designing hiding places. They built double walls, they made false ceilings, and they camouflaged attics and cellars. They hid Jews in factories and offices, in nunneries, monasteries, churches, and hospitals, in stables, cemeteries, pigsties, cowsheds, haystacks, pigeon coops, and greenhouses. When overcrowding inside the secret hideaways became a problem, Jews took turns standing, kneeling, squatting, sleeping. Small children were hidden in boxes, garbage bins, baskets, baking stoves.

Of course the Gestapo knew thousands were in hiding. They searched wherever they could, and got others to hunt out Jews for them. Non-Jews collaborated because they approved of the Nazi policy or they hated Jews. Some made a business out of informing, or accepted special favors in return. For turning in Jews the Gestapo paid off in rations of sugar, brandy, cigarettes, or in cash. The price for a human soul varied.

People caught hiding Jews paid a price too. They were usually shot on the spot, or hanged in a public place as a lesson to others who might hide Jews.

To what in a non-Jew could a Jew in that tragic time

appeal? Only to "feelings of mercy, compassion, loving kindness," writes Yehuda Bauer, a historian of the Holocaust. "In some places he met people who had these qualities; in most places he did not. He had no power at all to appeal to other sentiments on practical considerations. . . . The Jew was powerless, and the European background of antisemitism did not permit for more than a very partial reassertion of humanism in the attitude toward him." Yet, Bauer goes on: "In the darkness of Gentile attitudes to Jews there shone many bright lights. In places where the darkness was black indeed, the lights, though few, shone much brighter. In the end, beyond political and religious convictions, it was basic morality that counted."

We now know that it was possible to save Jews, for some Jews did survive the Holocaust. Again, we need to imagine ourselves back in those years, to understand how the people of that time perceived what was going on. The Nazis' vague threats of murder did not seem real to the Jews until *Kristallnacht*, toward the end of 1938. Even so, most German Jews still did not believe they were faced with total extinction until the summer of 1942, when word of mass murders in the woods beyond the ghettos and in the gas chambers finally filtered back to the surviving Jews; then the awakening began. (By that time the majority of Polish Jews were no longer alive.) But knowing is a gradual process. Information had to reach the Jews; then it had to be believed; then the mind had to see the connection between this terrible new reality and a possible way out. Only lastly *might* there come a decision to act—*might*, for even at this stage, not everyone was ready, or able, to act.

That is true also of the Gentiles, who had to face the reality of the mass murder of their Jewish fellow citizens. They had to hear of it, had to believe it, had to decide what to do about it. Some Gentiles in Germany did act—and became "bright lights" that shone in the blackest darkness.

Take Frau Schmidt, a washerwoman in the town of Kreuzen. She had worked for the family of a Jewish doctor for years. On *Kristallnacht* the doctor was arrested by the Gestapo and sent to the Dachau concentration camp. His wife and daughter, fearing they too would be picked up, hid in a friendly neighbor's apartment. Every day Frau Schmidt left a basket of food for them, even though her two sons were SS officers and would have turned their mother in for helping Jews.

Or take Christine and Robert, owners of a bakery in a small town. Earlier in the Nazi regime, when shopkeepers were forbidden to sell to Jews, they continued to bake challah on Fridays, and secretly delivered the bread to Jews late at night so they could celebrate the Shabbos meal.

In Nazi Germany all merchants were compelled to post signs saying "Jews Not Wanted Here." But some still let Jews buy from them secretly at night. Or Gentile neighbors of Jews sometimes bought extra amounts of food and other supplies at the market, with the unspoken understanding of the shopkeeper. Parcels of food were left on doorsteps or tossed through windows or across fences. Thus these good people helped keep their Jewish neighbors alive for a time—until deportation to the death camps claimed them.

Hans Hirschel, a forty-year-old Jew, was a scholar, author, and editor who went into hiding in Berlin early in 1942. He grew a beard and wore dark glasses as a disguise and was being hidden in an apartment by Maria von Maltzen, whom he called Marushka. She was a countess, descended from a family of old Swedish nobility that had migrated to Germany centuries before. Marushka loved Germany but hated the Nazis. She would do anything to end their evil. She had broken with her brother, an ardent Nazi, who had inherited the family estate. While working for her doctoral degree in science, she had helped two outspoken anti-Nazis, a priest and a professor, to evade arrest and flee Germany. She had been in the underground even before she met Hans.

In 1939 Marushka took up with Hans partly to defy the racial laws. But they soon fell deeply in love. After Hans faked a suicide to get the police off his trail, he moved into Marushka's small flat. In the flat was a massive boxlike bed. If anyone came to search for Jews, Hans could climb inside it, pull a lid over himself, and breathe through concealed air holes.

Hans ran the household and Marushka supported them both by working at a string of odd jobs and by trading on the black market. Her specialty was selling false documents—identity cards, ration cards, priority cards. Cooped up in the flat, Hans wrote articles, book reviews, radio plays, even short books—all assignments Marushka got, pretending she was writing them. Hans's work contained guarded criticism of the Nazis, which somehow they failed to detect. For companionship, Hans had two Scotch terriers Marushka bought for him.

Early on, two tragedies struck them. Hans's mother was deported to a concentration camp and certain death, and Marushka, pregnant by Hans, gave birth to a sickly infant boy who died after only a few days when an air raid cut off the electric power and the hospital's incubator failed. (A Swedish friend working in Berlin had pretended he was the baby's father.)

Sometimes Hans's lonely days were enlivened by other Jews who passed through the apartment on their way to refuge elsewhere. A knock on the door, and an "illegal" would enter, asking to stay for just a few nights till he or she could move on. It was best to shift around, keep your trail from getting too warm.

How did these Jews know Marushka's apartment was a refuge? Gradually Hans figured out that Marushka was part of the resistance movement in Berlin. Some nights she came home late or not at all, and would offer no explanation. Marushka had had no choice but to keep her illegal work secret from Hans. That way if the Gestapo caught him, he would have no information to reveal under torture.

But publicly Marushka was the Countess von Maltzen—a prized guest at the dinner parties of Berlin's upper circle. On those evenings she dined well, for a change, and gathered information useful to the resistance. It was not "resistance" in the usual form of sabotage or assassination. Rather it was the defense of people on the run— Jews, mostly, and some political dissidents.

Once Marushka escorted two disguised Jews out of Berlin by train and then led them into a forest where they boarded a freight train that a bribed engineer and crew had stopped on a desolate stretch of track. Two crates of furniture in a boxcar were carefully opened and emptied and the Jews put inside. The crates were sealed up, and then the train rolled on until it reached the port city of Lubeck. There the crates were loaded onto a freighter, and unloaded the next day in Nazi-free Sweden.

Most individuals who aided the German resistance movement could offer only a little money or a hiding place for a night or two. It was the German or Scandinavian church groups, with their larger networks, who often were able to be of the most help. Funds were raised abroad to bribe high SS officials to free certain people, many of them Jews. Marushka's tie was to the Church of Sweden in Berlin. She was accepted by the secret group there when the pastor learned that this countess, with great social and political connections, wanted to help people in trouble to get away. One of Marushka's co-workers was Eric Wesslen, a parish worker whose real job was to "buy back" people from the SS. Often Marushka was the one who learned of special persons picked up by the SS and promptly told Wesslen, who took the next step. Marushka's job was to find these people a place to hide while Wesslen arranged to get them out of Germany.

After being released by the SS, these people had to be provided not only with food and lodging but also with false papers to show they were authorized to live or work in Berlin. Marushka knew a Chinese printer who could forge papers. Then the documents had to bear official stamps. For a time Marushka did that herself by a process of lifting stamps from old documents bought on the black market or stolen—and transferring the stamps to the forged ones. Later the Swedes supplied her with a counterfeit stamp that worked perfectly.

The bombing of Berlin increased as the war ground on, and Marushka's work became even more risky. But the bombs wrecked police stations too, wiping out their records and making it easier to create new identities for Jews without papers.

As the city crumbled into ruins, many illegal Jews began to believe they would outlive the war. Penned up in cellars and attics and closets for so long, they became understandably careless. They took walks outdoors for the first time in years, sometimes only to be spotted and captured.

Once, two Gestapo men came to Marushka's flat, claiming they knew Jews hid there. They ransacked the place, then tried to open the bed, into which Hans had flung himself the second they heard the officers outside the door. When the lid wouldn't come off, they demanded Marushka open it. She angrily refused and dared them to fire a gun into it if they were so sure she was lying and someone was hiding there. But you'll pay for the fabric and repairs, she warned. They glared at her, hesitated, flustered by her confidence. Then turned away and left. Hans had heard everything, of course. He was so shaken he couldn't climb out of the bed without Marushka's help. She put out the signal at once that all illegals were to stay away from her flat. Hans had to leave.

Friends in the countryside agreed to shelter Hans. He slipped out the back through a concealed passage and evaded the men the Gestapo had posted. They kept watch for two more weeks, then quit. Hans came back home.

Marushka's work went on, amid the stench of unburied corpses that now lay in the Berlin streets after every air raid. Grave burial was no longer possible; bodies were burned on huge funeral pyres. By spring 1945 the Russians were on the edge of Berlin. Military supplies were moving

23

through the city's center by horse cart; Berlin had run out of gas. Dead horses littered the streets. At night starving Berliners crept out to butcher the horses for food. Anyone on the street who looked like an army deserter or whose papers seemed suspicious, the Nazis shot dead.

One night the shooting stopped. The war was over. Hans shaved off his beard. Soon after, he and Marushka were married.

Marushka's story is one of many that could be told. If not for the humanity of such Gentiles, many more Jews would have lost their lives. When the war ended, over 1,100 Jews came out of hiding in Berlin where their German neighbors had protected them. The Nazi racist creed had not swamped every German mind. SS records recovered long after the war report the mood of the Germans during Hitler's regime. These records seem to indicate, says Yehuda Bauer, that there was more "apathy, indifference, discomfort at the thought of what was happening to the Jews, and fear of the Nazi authorities, than . . . active agreement with Nazi policies."

Baltic
Sea

LITHUANIA
● Kovno
Vilna

EAST
PRUSSIA

● Minsk

POLAND
UNDER
GERMAN
RULE

Warsaw
●

● Lodz

Plaszow
Cracow
● ——Tarnopol
Auschwitz
● Lvov

SLOVAKIA

● Budapest

HUNGARY

RUMANIA
Bucharest ●

3 For Friends—or Strangers

What happened to Jews in Poland, the first country to be overrun by the German army? In scarcely three weeks the Nazis had Poland in an iron grip. To Hitler, the Poles were subhuman, fit for nothing but slavery. And the Jews among them were in an even lower category—bacilli.

In 1939, 10 percent of Poland's population was Jewish, 3.3 million people, the largest concentration of Jews in all Europe. Two million of Poland's Jews fell directly into the hands of the invading German army. (The rest came under Russian control when Joseph Stalin, under his pact with Hitler, invaded Poland from the east.) The two powers divided the country between themselves, and Poland no longer existed as a state. Two years later, by the end of the winter of 1941–1942, more than 90 percent of the Polish Jews trapped by the Germans were dead.

What determined the fate of the Jews during the Holocaust had much to do with how the Christians of each country felt about them. Poland's Jews were the least assimilated in Europe. Their appearance, their clothing, their behavior were different from those of Polish Christians. In part this was because Orthodox Polish Jews practiced a certain ritual and wore prescribed dress. Then, too, most Jews lived in cities, while most Poles lived in rural areas. Very few Jews farmed; the great majority worked for little money in industry or commerce. And for most Jews Yiddish, not Polish, was their first language.

In the prewar years all of Poland suffered great economic hardship. Her Jews, said the *London Jewish Chronicle* in 1937, are a "helpless minority sunk in squalid poverty and misery such as can surely be paralleled nowhere on the face of the earth." The lot of the Polish Jews was made worse by a huge wave of anti-Semitism that blamed them for all the nation's ills and took the form of economic boycotts, gross discrimination, and pogroms. Catholic priests—most of them anti-Semitic— charged Jews with corruption of Polish morals, thus adding to the Nazi poison. Political parties on the right called for the expulsion of all Jews; most Poles supported that proposal.

With the German invasion came an extensive new campaign of anti-Semitic propaganda, which made the Nazi policy of mass murder easier to carry out. Jews were locked behind ghetto walls and separated physically from their Christian neighbors. Poles were encouraged to loot Jewish homes and to take furniture, clothing, and anything else of value as the Jews were driven out. The Poles who profited had no desire to see the Jews return to claim their property.

Still, although anti-Semitism was widespread, betrayal and inhumanity all too common, a small minority did risk their lives to help their Jewish neighbors. It was the courage and generosity of this minority that enabled 43,000 Jews to find hiding places in Warsaw in 1942. It was much harder to help a Jew in Poland than it was in some other European countries. In Poland, if a single person helped a Jew, families and whole neighborhoods were punished for this "collective" guilt. Children were shot dead in front of their parents, and then the parents were executed. In one village the Nazis pushed thirty-three Poles and the Jews they were hiding into three houses and there burned them alive. In another village, where people had given food and shelter to about one hundred Jews hiding in the nearby forest, the Nazis set fire to the whole village, keeping the Poles inside their homes until they all died.

What Polish Christians did to rescue Jews must be seen against this background. First, they knew the Nazis would destroy anyone who tried to help. And second, any merciful gesture toward Jews invited the hostility and contempt of fearful neighbors, who might even turn them in to the Gestapo.

Take the story of Carola Sapetowa, a Christian villager who came to Cracow to work in the household of a Jewish family, the Hochheisers. When the Nazis invaded Poland, Mr. Hochheiser was shot and his wife and their three small children were locked up in the ghetto. On the day the Cracow ghetto was closed and all the Jews were put on transports for a death camp, Carola went to the gates of the ghetto to see once more the family she thought of as "my own." Mrs. Hochheiser spotted her and whispered to her two youngest children, the boy Samush and the girl Saliusha, "Go to Carolcha." The little ones slipped past the tall boots of the SS guards and into Carola's arms.

Carola left Cracow and took the two children home to her village, where her father welcomed them all. She kept the children indoors, but when neighbors found she was hiding Jews, they threatened her. Hand them over to the Gestapo, they said, or the village will be burned and we'll all be killed. If you don't do it, we'll kill them ourselves. She silenced them for a time with bribes. But the hounding began again. One day Carola put Samush and Saliusha in a wagon and drove openly through the village, telling the peasants she was going to drown the children. They believed her. That night she sneaked them back and paid a neighbor to let her hide them in his hayloft. During the long hot months of summer the children stayed there, and were fed secretly. They grew sick from the airless dark, the dust, and the fear. When Carola ran out of money to pay for that hiding place, she hid them in her father's stable until the end of the war. When Carola learned that Mrs. Hochheiser and her oldest child had died in a camp, she raised the children as her own.

Several Gentile women with the courage of Carola helped save a Jewish man we know only as "Kh.K." In the fall of 1942, during the mass shooting of Jews in Poland, Kh.K. lost his mother, two sisters, two nieces, and other relatives in the murder. How he himself survived we learn from testimony taken down after the war:

On the fourth of September, 1942, a Gentile woman named Kuzaniak—she was a neighbor of ours from before the war—told me not to let them take me to Bubasko [a town] because they were bringing us there to die. She found this out from her son who was a gendarme and she told me I must escape. She also said that because of my blond hair I could pass for a Gentile. I did what she told me—I jumped off the wagon that was leading us to extermination. Night was falling; I ran into the fields with my girl friend, Rukhl Sheyves. We walked through them till we came to the fields called Lasy Pod-karpackie. A Christian woman, Stanislawa Laskowska, took pity on me. She lived in the village of Dlugie. Before the war, she used to come to our store to buy material. At first, this Gentile woman hid me in her barn for ten days and then I went into the stable for a long time. She brought me food.

When there were raids or searches in the village, she sent me into the woods, but she left me food, hiding it where I could get it at night. When the weather held, I hid under the forest trees, but in the winter, I hid out in a cave. When the Christian woman was told there would be no trouble for a while, she took me into her home; I washed myself there. I even slept in the same bed with her. She made many sacrifices for me. In uncertain times, when I lay hidden in the stable with only a piece of bread wrapped in a kerchief, the mice crawled all over me and finished the bread before me.

Once, while I was hiding in the forest with a group of ten people, we were ambushed. It was during a raging blizzard—it was freezing cold and the snows were very deep. I only managed to get one shoe on before I ran away from there. Because of this, half of two toes on my right foot froze off. I had no bandages but I kept my foot in a rag and kept it on from January till April. It was only then I tried taking the rag off. As I did, pieces of my toe came off. The Gentile woman Laskowska now took care of me. Because of her goodness, I survived the Khorbn [Holocaust]. Afterwards, I had to wander over many areas before I was liberated.

Sometimes it was Jewish friends that Gentile rescuers helped, but some risked their lives for strangers too. One old Polish farmer gave shelter to a Jew he knew. When the Jew asked if he would hide others of his family, the farmer couldn't deny him. They in turn pleaded with the farmer to hide some of their friends. The number the farmer hid grew and grew. Finally he ended up with twenty-two people in his care. All of them survived.

Jewish children were special targets of the Nazis. Hitler saw the next generation as the promise (or threat) of a Jewish future. One and a half million Jewish children under the age of twelve were gassed in the death camps or otherwise deliberately killed, many of them before the eyes of their parents. But some children were saved by their Gentile teachers, nurses, housemaids, or servants. Or by total strangers. When deportation of the Jews began in the small town of Mordy, a Polish woman, Elizabeth Przewlocka, snatched a Jewish child she didn't know while the Nazi guard wasn't looking, and hid him safely until she was able to get him into a Polish orphanage in Warsaw.

Another Gentile, Juliana Larish, ran a meat supply business in Warsaw and used most of its profits to help Jews in hiding. She concealed ten Jews in her own house and gave them more than just shelter: She brought in big baskets of food, as well as clothing and books. To divert suspicion about the large amounts of food she carried home regularly, Juliana often invited her Polish and German customers to come to her house for a snack. Through the thin walls of their hidden chamber the silent Jews could hear the talk around table, including the vicious anti-Semitic remarks. Once Juliana's employees told the Gestapo they suspected she was sheltering Jews and her house was raided. But she was too careful to leave damaging evidence around. The Gestapo raid did not scare her; she continued to help Jews until the war ended. In all she saved the lives of twenty-one Jews.

The particular acts of some rescuers are almost beyond belief. Pero, a middle-aged clerk in a Warsaw hotel, is one example. A Jewish woman, Malie Piotrskovska, and her thirteen-year-old daughter Bronka, lost their hiding places one day and had to walk the streets in a frantic search for another. Gentile youngsters denounced them as Jews, and they were taken to the Gestapo. There the two produced false documents attesting that they were Gentiles. They managed to answer, however haltingly, questions testing their knowledge of Christianity. The Germans were not convinced. They said they must produce a Pole who could vouch for their being Christian, or they would be killed.

Pero was the only Polish friend who might help them. They gave his phone number, and the Gestapo called him to say they were holding two women suspected of being Jewish, which they denied. Would he come in and vouch for them tomorrow morning?

Malie and Bronka spent a terrible night in their cell. Would Pero dare come? He did, and was grilled by the Gestapo. He stuck by his friends, insisting he had known them as Christians since well before the war. The Germans reminded him that the penalty for lying was death. Pero assured them he was not taking such a risk, for he knew they were good Christians. At last he convinced the Gestapo and the two women were released. If you have any trouble in the future with such false charges, the Gestapo told Malie, report it to us. We'll take care of it. Pero took the two women into his own home. Later he gave shelter to other Jews.

Even a Pole saturated in anti-Semitism might offer help

to a Jew. The teenage daughter of a poor blacksmith, out walking one day, noticed someone entangled in barbed wire lying in a ditch. The girl came closer and saw that it was a Jewish woman, alive and in need of help. She ran home for wire cutters, released the woman, and brought her to her parents. They took the Jew in, hiding her from the villagers. The Gentile family grew fond of their "guest," especially the teenage girl, who lovingly spoke of the woman as "my foundling."

But neighbors grew suspicious. If exposed, the whole family would die. Rather than abandon the Jew, the parents decided she should leave the village with their daughter, whose typically Polish looks might protect them both. So they moved from place to place, managing somehow to survive. One day the woman asked the girl how she felt about Jews. The quick answer came:

"Oh, I hate them! The Jews are horrible. They are dirty thieves. They cheat everybody. Jews are a real menace. For Passover they catch Christian children, murder them, and use their blood for matzo."

The Jewish woman tried hard to show how false these accusations were. Of course *you're* not like that, the girl said. But all the other Jews are. The woman burst into tears. The girl hugged her close and said, "Please don't cry; it hurts my heart to see you so unhappy. You know that you are dearer to me than a sister. But you must understand that I sucked these stories with my mother's milk. Can you expect me to give them up?"

Nevertheless, no matter how strong her prejudice, the girl went on to help other Jewish strangers.

There were other women who helped. Sophia was one. She hid several Jewish women in her Warsaw home, where each passed as her nurse, seamstress, cook, or maid. She turned her home into an operation headquarters for the Jews in the armed underground. She got friends in the post office to unseal mail addressed to the Gestapo and destroy any letters from informers reporting Jews in hiding.

Several Gentile women served the Jewish fighting groups, acting as liaison between them and the outside world or carrying messages from one ghetto to another. Jadzia Duniec, a young Catholic courier for the Jews, was captured by the Nazis and executed. Two women in their seventies, Janina Plawczynska and Rena Laterner, carried messages between the Jewish and Polish fighters in Warsaw. When the ghetto uprising was crushed, they hid ten Jews and, when they were caught, died alongside them.

While some Gentiles devoted their energies to helping Jews in the ghettos, others helped Jews who were doing forced labor in factories or labor camps. Zygmunt Rostal came from a large Polish working-class family and often suffered hunger because of chronic unemployment in Poland. The members of his close-knit family were political radicals, and when a teenager Zygmunt joined a left-wing youth group. It was one of the few in Poland that welcomed Jews, and Zygmunt was labeled a "Jew lover" by his classmates.

During the war Zygmunt took a job in an ammunition plant so he could help Jews doing forced labor there. As a Gentile he was free to move about the plant. He used his freedom to supply Jews with food and medicine. When he learned about Nazi plans that affected Jews, he passed the news on to his underground contacts. But Zygmunt felt his most important task was to try to give heart to the desperate and depressed Jewish workers, for those who gave up all hope and sank into listless apathy were shot by the Germans for being useless. Three times Zygmunt was caught doing something for a Jew, and each time he was beaten badly. But he kept on trying until the Nazis shut down the factory.

Irene was nineteen when the Germans invaded Poland. Working in a hospital, she was captured by the Germans and sent to Tarnopol where, because she spoke German, she was made to serve meals to the German officers and staff. Separated from her family, and lonely, Irene made friends with twelve Jewish prisoners who washed clothes for the Germans. Their Jewishness made no difference to her: "We were all in trouble and we had a common enemy." Whatever she learned from the Germans she passed on to the Jews, who got word into the ghetto. Her warnings of coming Nazi raids helped save the lives of many Jews who managed to escape to hiding places in time.

As the ghetto was emptied by death and deportation, her twelve Jewish friends escaped and asked her for help. She had no space to hide them in her tiny one-room apartment. She prayed to God for help, and the next morning, "like a miracle," an aging German major asked her to keep house for him in the large villa he occupied. She took the job, arranging for the twelve Jews to enter the house by a coal chute and hide in the cellar. There they stayed for weeks, with Irene feeding them secretly.

One night the major came home unexpectedly and found Jews in the kitchen with Irene. He couldn't believe his eyes. The Germans had just hanged several Polish families in the town square, together with the Jewish families they had helped. He dragged Irene into his office and yelled at her. He had trusted her, protected her. How could she do this terrible thing?

Irene said, "I know only one thing. They're my friends. I had to do it. I did not have a home to take them to. I don't have a family. Forgive me, but I would do it again. Nobody has a right to kill and murder because of religion or race."

"But you know what can happen to you," he replied. They had both witnessed the hangings in the square. By now Irene was in tears. Then he relented. "I cannot do that to you," he said. "I cannot let you die." So he let them all stay. Soon afterward the major had to leave, for the Germans were retreating. Irene and the Jews fled into the forest, and three days later the Russian army arrived. They were free of the Nazis at last.

Such people as Irene saw Jews not as Jews, but simply as people struggling to stay alive. It wasn't a Jew who asked for help—at least not the Jew of the anti-Semitic stereotype—but a desperate, persecuted human being. And if he or she was a stranger, it made no difference. Aron Blum, alone, with no documents, no money, no hope, knocked at Frank Dworski's door. Blum tells what happened:

When I came to his house he did not know me at all. In fact, I did not even know the man who directed me to him. As a welcome he said, "Bread in this house you will not miss." He was as poor as I was, but he shared all. He simply looked upon this help as the most natural thing. He had so much heart and courage. He made papers for me, found me a job, and gave me shelter. After a while, and upon my request, he travelled to Lvov to

37

bring a friend of mine, also a Jew. To make this possible for my friend he arranged false papers. On the way the train was searched by the Nazis. It was customary in such situations to throw away all incriminating evidence. Not he. He hid the papers. Dworski was not afraid, even though he knew that he could die for it. But he also knew that, without these papers, he could not bring my friend back, and that this in turn could cost my friend his life. Dworski had courage and luck. All went well. He brought my friend, whom he kept in his house as he did everyone else who turned to him. All this he did without ever receiving, or expecting to receive, anything in return.

4   The Sin of Hiding Jews

How their Christian neighbors felt about them, historians agree, was one of the important influences on the fate of Europe's Jews during the Holocaust. Let's look at Eastern Europe again. We've just examined Poland. What about the many other countries in that huge region of Nazi occupation? The situation varied. But from the evidence we can say that, by and large, the local populations were hostile to the Jews and even cooperated with the Nazis against them. Thousands of Jews—unarmed civilians as well as armed partisans—died because they were betrayed by non-Jews. A sizeable part of the people of Eastern Europe were ready and willing to get rid of the Jews. What was said in Chapter 3 about the history of Christian-Jewish relations in Poland is generally true for most of Eastern Europe. Anti-Semitism was strong and deep-rooted in the vast majority of the population. By agreement with the Germans the Soviet army occupied the independent Baltic countries—Lithuania, Latvia, and Estonia—in September 1939. But when Hitler broke his pact with Stalin in 1941 and attacked Russia, the Soviet armies withdrew from these countries. Even before the

Germans could occupy that region, large numbers of Jews in Lithuania were murdered by Lithuanians. The same thing happened when the German army entered Latvia and other parts of former Soviet territory. Nazi officers reported that the local people were "reliable and invaluable from the start" in exterminating "Bolsheviks and Jews."

Along with the German armies came a flood of anti-Jewish propaganda. The Germans took full advantage of the deep resentment of the peasants against Communist rule. Nazi propaganda linked the grievances of the people with anti-Semitism. Jews and Communists are one and the same, it was charged; get rid of the one and you get rid of the other. The Nazi propaganda was welcomed in the collaborationist press of Eastern Europe, and in many places anti-Jewish pogroms followed. The Ukrainians took the initiative in setting up concentration camps for Jews. Their civil officials issued anti-Jewish decrees, proposed "actions" against the Jews to the Nazi authorities, and upon approval carried them out.

It would take a powerfully independent spirit to resist not only the Nazis but also the anti-Semitism of the local population. Still, there were many examples of aid given by Christians to Jews. Sometimes it was belief in a minority faith that strengthened rescuers. The small Baptist minority in the Ukraine, who lived scattered throughout the countryside, did much to help Jews. The Baptists too were persecuted for their faith and reached out to the Jews no matter what the risk.

Although the Ukraine was Soviet territory, the Soviets took no positive steps to defend Jews or rescue them. Many in the government were themselves infected with anti-Semitism, as was much of the Russian population. Soviet leaders said their prime task was fighting off the German invaders, who were slaughtering everyone in their path, not only Jews. If the Soviets beat back the Germans, that would help the Jews to survive, they argued. When the Nazis had first moved into Eastern Europe, about 400,000 Polish and Baltic Jews fled into the USSR. They were given no special treatment, nor could they have been, in the general disaster of early Soviet defeats. Masses of those Jews died of hunger and disease. Some 250,000 survived.

The Nazis formed auxiliary police units of Latvians, Lithuanians, Belorussians, and Ukrainians. They were used as guards in concentration camps in their own districts or in Poland, and shared in the looting and murdering of Jews. Protests against such bloodletting were made by some small local groups, but the Gestapo quickly silenced them.

It took a rare heroism to stand up against mass murder. One such heroic man was the Greek Orthodox Archbishop of Lvov, Andrew Sheptitsky. An old man, paralyzed and confined to a wheelchair, Sheptitsky denounced the German invaders as barbarians and issued a pastoral letter titled "Thou Shalt Not Murder!" When many Ukrainians joined Nazis in murdering Jews, he threatened "divine punishment" for any who would "shed innocent blood and make of themselves outcasts of human society by disregarding the sanctity of man." He banned religious services for all who accepted Hitler's gospel of murder.

When an official from the German Foreign Ministry came to see Sheptitsky, he boldly condemned the Germans' inhumane attitude toward the Jews. In Lvov alone they had killed 100,000. A Ukrainian youngster had confessed to him that in one night he had killed seventy-five Jews. This is intolerable! Sheptitsky told the official.

But he went beyond words. He hid Jewish children and adults in his church, stored the Torah scrolls there, and arranged for 150 other Jews to be concealed in convents. Although hundreds of monks and nuns knew of the Jews' presence, not a single Jew was betrayed. To one Jew whom he concealed, disguised as a monk, the archbishop said, "I want you to be a good Jew, and I am not saving you for your own sake. I am saving you for your people. I do not expect any reward, nor do I expect you to accept my faith."

His ringing voice reached many Ukrainian people—peasants, housemaids, workers, who in turn saved or helped Jews. In several districts, where small towns and villages were surrounded by thick forests, hundreds of Jews escaped to the woods and formed armed groups. The foresters—mostly Ukrainian peasants—kept the Jews informed of Nazi raids and provided them with food and weapons.

Some years after the war, a survivor of the Holocaust, "MG," recorded his experiences under the Nazi occupation of the Ukraine. When the Germans took over his shtetl, local Ukrainians butchered whole Jewish families with pitchforks and spades. Then they helped German soldiers kill 300 Red Army men captured nearby. Soviet soldiers represented to them the Communist regime they hated. The Germans rounded up many of the remaining Jews for hard labor and sent the others off to the camps. MG, then about twenty-five, escaped with a few friends to the village of Miszkowice. Koliwicki, a Pole, was in charge of a large farm there that supplied food for the Germans. The Pole took them in and gave them work, food, and a place to sleep. MG's brother and sister came to work on the farm with him. A year later the Germans ordered that all Jews in Miszkowice be rounded up and sent to the Tarnopol ghetto. MG and his brother and sister decided not to let themselves be taken. Koliwicki agreed to let them hide on the farm. MG tells what happened:

We stole into one of the barns on the manor, dug a pit under a stack of hay, and stayed down there for six months. One night a week we came up and went to the caretaker's cottage. His wife left out a large bowl of food—barley or potatoes—with some bread, so we had enough to eat. We never met the caretaker's wife and she didn't look out at us when we came in the night. We were terrified walking to and from the caretaker's home for food. Peasants came all the time to bale hay from the stack we were hiding under. Once, they got so close they were just one motion away from uncovering us. We dove into another pile of hay and hid there. We still came to the Pole's door during the nights, and his wife left the food out for us like always.

One Shabbos morning, while we were lying under the hay in the new hiding place, young peasant couples came in to do some threshing. They started taking apart the stacks of wheat we were hiding behind. Just as they were about to find us, I, myself, called to a Ukrainian peasant, Shudlovski, I knew before the war. I told him we were hiding here and not to give us away. The peasant quickly called over the old foreman, the Ukrainian Sechko, and we asked him to help us. He threw some hay over us and moved the peasant couples off to another spot, away from where we were hiding.

Then, one winter morning, German soldiers and Ukrainian police swooped down on the farm to grab field hands for labor in Germany. MG's family ran off into the forest before they could be caught. Guards shot at them and peasants refused to take them in. They hid in stables, sneaked past villages, froze in the terrible cold. Finally they were so hopeless they decided to enter the Tarnopol ghetto voluntarily. Just then they came across a poor Ukrainian peasant, Mishko Kormilo, and told him they meant to give themselves up. He talked them out of it, and said he'd hide them in the loft of his shed. He spread his ten bales of hay for them, and got them food:

We lay in hiding in the loft for eight days when we suddenly heard there'd been a burglary at the manor where Kormilo worked as foreman. He was suspected and police came to search his hut. They climbed up into the loft looking for stolen goods near where we were hiding. The police overturned the whole attic but didn't touch the ten bales of straw where me and my brother and sister were hiding.

After this scare, Kormilo wouldn't let us stay any longer. His wife and mother hated the Jews and badgered him for letting us hide here. Kormilo smuggled us into the manor where we worked earlier. He took us down and hid us in the ice cellar. We lay there for three days and nights stretched out on the ice. All we had to eat was frozen ice. On the third day, a peasant woman came down to the cellar and spotted us. She was an old Ukrainian maid. When she saw us lying like that on the ice, she started crying and took pity on us. She brought us some food right away.

Afraid they'd be found now, they left the cellar and went back to Kormilo again. He took them in once more, and hid them in a covered pit under the floor of his hut, where he kept potatoes during the winter. Kormilo's wife and mother knew they were hiding there, but began to treat them kindly, bringing them food. To conceal his "sin" of hiding Jews, Kormilo would go about the village ranting against the evil people who hid Jews. They stayed in that hole until the Russians liberated the district. Then they walked back to their hometown. They found themselves to be among the few Jews who had survived.

Another Ukrainian, Alexander Kryvoiaza, employed fifty-eight Jews in his factory and hid them during anti-Jewish raids. Occasionally, women, former maids in Jewish homes, helped save their employers. Ivan Bubik, the mayor of Buczacz, saved many Jews and managed to keep the Nazis from establishing a ghetto in his town.

How many "good Gentiles" were there in the Ukraine? There is no way of knowing exactly. But one indication is an official SS report which lists some one hundred Ukrainians executed for helping or concealing Jews. This suggests there were far more, when you consider that only some were caught, some were given lighter sentences, and many others were shot on the spot and never entered the record. And the list covers only nine months and is limited to one part of the Ukraine.

In Lithuania, Latvia, and Estonia, almost 150,000 Jews

were murdered within three months of the Nazi invasion. The Germans got local Nazis to take the lead. A Lithuanian journalist, Klimatis, organized 300 men into a band of killers. In a few days in Kaunas they massacred 3,500 Jews, destroyed several synagogues, and burned sixty houses in a Jewish neighborhood. The grateful Germans praised the gang for "doing particularly well in extermination actions."

Other bands of volunteer killers did much the same to help the Nazis wipe out "useless and undesirable people." Church leaders were appalled. "Are we to be Europe's hangmen?" they asked in a leaflet. An underground newspaper warned the Lithuanians: "It should be clear to all that the German aim is to destroy the Lithuanian people. First they attempt to destroy us morally, taking pains to turn all Lithuanians into executioners. Later the Germans will shoot us as they do the Jews, and will justify their acts to the world by saying that Lithuanians are depraved hangmen and sadists."

Such voices were all too few in that country. Collaborators, informers, and assassins found their true calling in aiding the Nazis. But other Lithuanians risked their lives to save Jews. Joseph Stokauskas, director of Vilna's archival office, hid Jews who had escaped the ghetto. A sizeable group of scholars and professors worked together to hide Jews, especially children. Sometimes it took their combined efforts to rescue a single person or family. A Jewish botanist in Vilna, Professor Movshowitch, had to be concealed in four successive homes as the Nazis sniffed his trail. Peasants, artisans, teachers, clergymen—to every kind of person Jews owed their survival.

Several priests in Vilna gave sermons against taking

Jewish property or shedding Jewish blood. The Gestapo seized them all. A priest who tried to help a Jewish girl by baptizing her was caught, flogged, and sent into forced labor. In the town of Vidukle, the Germans rounded up the 200 Jews and locked them into the synagogue to be murdered. The local priest, Jonas, managed to smuggle thirty children out and hide them in his church. When an informer reported this to the Germans, they demanded the priest hand over the children. He stood in their way, crying, "If you kill the children, you will have to kill me first!" They did, and then shot the children.

In a diary kept from mid-1941 to mid-1943, while he lived within the Vilna ghetto, Herman Kruk noted from time to time the decency of some Christians:

SEPTEMBER 7, 1941. Christians come to the ghetto, bringing bread and clothing. The Christians weep more than the Jews. . . .

MAY 15, 1942. I read a letter from a German to a Jewish girl. He is ready to help her in every possible way. He pleads with her not to treat him as a German. "Write to me. I am at your service." The letter concludes with the words: "Destroy the letter at once. Herbert."

It was to the Vilna Ghetto that Anna Simaite came, a heroic non-Jew whose capacity to love and sacrifice and fight can never be forgotten. She was Lithuanian, raised by her grandfather to reject bigotry and anti-Semitism. She was a librarian at Vilna University and an eminent literary critic when the war broke out. She could have remained silent about the destruction of the Jews. Instead

49

she said: "When the Germans forced Jews of Vilna into a ghetto, I could no longer go on with my work. I could not remain in my study. I could not eat. I was ashamed that I was not Jewish myself. I had to do something. I realized the danger involved, but it could not be helped. A force much stronger than myself was at work."

To help Jews was only to be human. Anna Simaite decided to get into the ghetto to offer her help. But how? Using the pretext that she wanted to gather up the many valuable books Jewish students had borrowed from her library, she persuaded the Germans to give her a pass. Once inside the ghetto she absorbed the feverish life around her. She found Jews staging plays, conducting concerts, running schools, attending lectures and art exhibits. Here were a people sentenced to death by starvation and torture and deportation, yet they spent their remaining hours celebrating life.

She worked out several ways to save Jewish lives. She urged people to risk taking in adult Jews whose escape from the ghetto could be arranged, and she found hiding places for Jewish children spirited out of the ghetto. She got forged identity papers for Jews. She smuggled out letters from leaders of the underground and precious scraps of diaries kept by ghetto dwellers. She used her own ration cards only for potatoes and cabbage. All the rest—for bread, marmalade, margarine, cheese—she gave to ghetto children. When the Jews prepared to make a last stand against the Nazis, she smuggled in small arms and ammunition. With each such act Anna Simaite took a step closer to death.

At last, in the summer of 1944, she was arrested by the Gestapo for forging Aryan papers for a ten-year-old girl. They beat her; they starved her; they tortured her. But she betrayed no secrets. She was sentenced to death. Then friends at the university bribed a high Nazi official to commute her sentence. She was shipped to the camp at Dachau, and then to another one in southern France. There, close to dying, she was liberated by the Allied armies.

Not far from the Vilna ghetto was a Benedictine convent where seven nuns were living at the time of the Nazi occupation. The mother superior could not put out of her thoughts the suffering of the Jews walled up so close by. She called the sisters together to decide what they might do. Soon after, a few nuns were let into the ghetto by unsuspecting guards. Inside, they made contact with the underground and worked out ways of getting Jews out and hiding them in the convent and elsewhere. The small convent was at one time overflowing with the "nuns," some of them looking rather masculine.

When the ghetto formed a fighters' unit, the mother superior offered to smuggle in weapons. She and her nuns scoured the countryside for pistols, grenades, bayonets, daggers, knives. They became experts in explosives. Still, the mother superior felt she was not doing enough. She wanted to go to the ghetto and fight alongside the Jews she considered brothers and sisters. But they insisted she was far too valuable an ally on the Aryan side. The ghetto was wiped out, but the survivors who had escaped earlier never forgot the heroism of the seven nuns.

Bulgaria is a small East European country bordering on the Black Sea. It had an ancient community of some 50,000 Sephardic Jews, about 1 percent of the population. They were mostly lower middle class or artisans, who lived in political and economic freedom but were segregated from the rest of society. They played no large part in cultural or political life.

Bulgaria allied itself with Germany in World War II, because a Fascist government under King Boris was in power and it hoped to regain territories Bulgaria had lost during World War I. The Germans did not take control over Bulgaria's internal affairs, but they pressed for anti-Jewish actions, and the Bulgarian government introduced measures to take away the property of Jews and concentrate them for deportation.

The Bulgarian people felt that native Jews were also Bulgarians, and several groups—the Orthodox Church, the professional classes, the unions, the Communist underground movement, even some government officials—protested the anti-Jewish moves. In Sofia, the capital, Christian workers marched in the streets to denounce anti-Jewish edicts, and several were killed for it by the police that night.

Mass conversions took place, with priests falsifying dates and marrying thousands of Christians to Jews to shield them from racist decrees. The priests were punished by the government for their daring, but they continued to defend Jews. When the Nazis increased their pressure on the government, it tried to appease them and save the native Bulgarian Jews by deporting only "foreign" Jews, meaning those who lived in Macedonia and Thrace, regions recently annexed from Greece and Yugoslavia. The head of the Orthodox Church stepped in to try to halt this move. He was joined by Dmitri Pleshev, Vice President of the Parliament.

Their protests failed. Over 11,000 Jews deported from Macedonia and Thrace died in Polish camps. By this time the Germans had begun to suffer defeats. Perhaps King Boris felt that he shouldn't make things worse than they need be. He responded to the public protests against mass murder by ordering that all Jewish deportations be stopped.

Soon after, King Boris died, mysteriously, and a new government took over. In January 1944 the Allies began mass bombing of Bulgaria. The new regime, seeing German power weaken, tried to break away from Hitler, first by declaring its neutrality, and then, going even further, by declaring war on Germany. In August, as the Red Army neared the Bulgarian border, the cabinet announced it had revoked all anti-Jewish laws.

Although the Bulgarian leadership did agree to the deportation of over 11,000 Jews from Macedonia and Thrace, it nevertheless succeeded in preventing the deportation of any native Jews from Old Bulgaria. It was an extraordinary outcome for the Jews, for in other Nazi-occupied lands the deportation and murder continued to the last possible moment.

LITHUANIA

● Kovno

Vilna ●

EAST
PRUSSIA

● Berlin

POLAND
UNDER
GERMAN
RULE

Warsaw
●

● Lodz

Plaszow
Cracow

Prague

● ― Tarnopol
BOHEMIA ●
MORAVIA ● ●
● Auschwitz ● Lvov

● Brinnlitz

SLOVAKIA

Vienna ●

● Budapest

HUNGARY

● Zagreb

CROATIA

● Belgrade

SERBIA

● Sofia

5 Schindler's Jews

Oskar Schindler: drinker, womanizer, gambler, prof-
iteer, briber, wheeler-dealer, Nazi. It does not read like
the description of a saint. Nor was he one. Yet he saved
human souls, 1,200 of them. Where did he come from?
How did he become a man of honor?

Oskar was born in 1908, in the small industrial city of
Zwittau, then part of the Austrian empire. (Ten years
later, after World War I, it became part of the new nation
of Czechoslovakia.) His father owned a farm machinery
plant and Oskar was trained to be an engineer. The Schindler family was Catholic, but young Oskar cared little
about religion. Among his friends were a few Jewish classmates at the German grammar school. More interested
in racing, Oskar built his own motorcycle and competed
on mountain courses.

At the age of twenty, he married Emilie, a gentleman
farmer's daughter. She was a quiet girl schooled in a convent. They seemed to have little in common. But who
could resist tall, handsome Oskar? His magnetic charm
was always successful with women. Now of draft age,
Oskar was called into military service. He detested every-

thing about it except the chance to drive a truck. After completing his service, he went home again and he worked for his father. But the factory went bankrupt during the depression of the 1930s. Oskar glided right into a job as a sales manager of an electrical company. He liked going out on the road, selling, meeting new people—especially women. What made his job easier was joining the local Nazi party. The Nazi badge helped get orders when he visited German companies.

In 1938 Hitler's troops marched into Czechoslovakia. Being a Nazi didn't look so good to Oskar now. He was shocked by the brutal way the Germans forcibly removed Jews and Czechs from those areas considered German and their grabbing of Czech and Jewish property. His wife Emilie thought Hitler would surely be punished for making himself God; his father believed Hitler, like Napoleon, would wind up a nobody. Oskar began to lose his zeal for the new order.

One evening, at a party, Oskar met a pleasant young German who talked business and politics with him as they drank alone in a side room. Growing confident with Oskar, the man identified himself as an officer in the Abwehr, the German Intelligence corps. You travel in Poland for your company, he said; why not supply the Abwehr with military and industrial information about that region? You'll be excused from military service, of course, if you become our agent. That made the proposal quite attractive to Oskar. He didn't worry about a military takeover of Poland. Not then.

A year later the invasion of Poland succeeded easily. And soon after, Oskar arrived in Cracow, a beautiful medieval city of Poland, ringed by metal, textile, and chemical plants. There he took charge of a factory that would make mess kits and field kitchenware for the German army.

Oskar settled comfortably into an elegant neighborhood of Cracow, his expensive clothes and sleek chauffered car matching the high style of his apartment. While his wife Emilie stayed at home in Moravia, he kept house with a German mistress and conducted an affair with his Polish secretary at the factory office.

Only a short distance from Cracow was the forced labor camp at Plaszow, the barbed-wire home of 20,000 Jews. Oskar was friendly with its chief, Amon Goeth, as well as with the district heads of the various Nazi security forces. Oskar once had been a salesman. Now in Cracow he was a tycoon, operating in a boom time. The contracts he got to manufacture the products that the German forces needed brought in big profits. Oskar worked inside a corrupt and savage system and knew how to use its every rotten device for his own ends. He dealt cleverly on the black market, enjoying a talent for acquiring luxuries— silk, furniture, jewelry, clothing, liquor. Some for himself, some to seduce Nazis in high places. Their friendship kept him out of the army. Why waste such a generous man on the battlefield?

But as Oskar saw the sporadic Nazi raids and killing of Jews increase, his "friends" began to rouse a deep disgust in him. He knew how the SS would sweep into a Jewish street, break into apartments, loot them of all they contained, rip jewelry off fingers and throats, break an arm or a leg of anyone who hid something, shoot anyone they pleased. One day an SS squad invaded a fourteenth-century synagogue. They lined up the Jews they found at prayer, dragged in Jewish passersby, and made them all file past the Torah and spit on it. When one Jew refused to spit on the scroll, they shot him. Then they shot all the others and burned down Poland's oldest synagogue. As the silent aim of the Nazis—to exterminate all the Jews—became clear to Oskar, a cold rage seized him. Were these German massacres of Jews the actions of a *civilized* nation? What could end this madness?

When Oskar took over the Cracow factory it had only forty-five workers. As his army contracts swelled, their number grew to 250. His accountant was a Jew, Itzhak Stern. Stern asked him to hire this Jewish friend, then that one, then still another, and soon Oskar had 150 Jews in his employ. In the spring of 1941 the Nazis ordered all Jews out of Cracow, all but five or six thousand skilled ones needed for the war effort. These were shoved behind ghetto walls. Oskar's plant became a haven for Jews claiming such skills. Those who worked for Oskar had a blue sticker that enabled them to go in and out of the ghetto to work.

A little later Oskar made a deal with the German armaments people to add a munitions section to his plant to make antitank shells. This was better than making only pots and pans, for now who could question that he had a really essential industry?

Oskar added a night shift, and took on more Jews. "You'll be safe working here," he told them. "If you work here, you'll live through the war." How could they believe that promise? Who was this young blond giant—he was only thirty-four—who made such promises? But Oskar's calm certainty made them believe. And they wanted to, of course.

58

Oskar went on making his deals. And through his close connections with the local Nazi hierarchy, he often learned of their plans and passed the information on to the Jews who worked for him. He did business with the SS man who ran the ghetto, Julian Scherner. Scherner liked women, booze, luxuries, all the good things that came with his new power. And he seemed to prefer working the Jews to killing them. Oskar made good use of Scherner to get still more Jews onto his work rolls.

When rumors started to fly that the ghetto would gradually be "eliminated," Oskar convinced Scherner to let him set up cots in his plant so his night shift wouldn't be interrupted. That got some of his Jews out of the ghetto. But many others were still inside.

One day Oskar learned that a number of his workers, including his office manager, Abraham Bankier, had been taken out of the ghetto along with a great many other Jews and marched off to the railroad. Oskar drove at once to the depot, and found the Jews boarding a long string of cattle cars. Bound for where? For what? No one seemed to know. A labor camp, someone guessed. Oskar had recently seen an SS bulletin asking for bids to build crematoria in Belzec, a camp southeast of Lublin. Could this be the destination of these Jews? He ran down the track, calling out Bankier's name. He found him and the other twelve of his workers huddled together in the corner of one car. Then, by bluff and bribe, he got the SS to scratch the thirteen names off the shipping list on the grounds that a mistake had been made about these essential munitions workers.

As Oskar watched Jews taken out of the ghetto and marched to the cattle cars, he could not fail to guess what the end would be. The proof came when Bachner, a young Jewish pharmacist who had been shipped off, returned to the ghetto eight days later. He had seen the final horror. The Cracow Jews had been taken to Belzec, stripped naked, their heads shaved, and forced into "bathhouses," where they were gassed. All but him. Somehow he had gotten to a latrine and dropped into its pit, hiding there three days in human waste up to his neck. At last he was able to climb out in the dark and slip out of the camp. Because the Cracow ghetto was the only home he knew, he had walked the tracks right back into it. Now everyone in the ghetto knew the truth.

Twice in 1942 Oskar was arrested by the Gestapo on suspicion of wrongdoing. But each time he was sprung from prison by his influential friends, and he went on protecting the Jews in his factory. Their living and working conditions were humane. They were spared the atrocities of the Plaszow labor camp, and whenever the SS ordered a few of his Jews to Plaszow, he always found a way to rescue them. His generosity to SS officials on their birthdays became legendary.

Oskar's factory now employed 550 Jews, for whose labor he paid the SS a fixed rate of so much per day per person. In the autumn of 1942 a Zionist courier came to see Oskar. Someone (perhaps Itzhak Stern) had sent word abroad to Jewish organizations that Oskar was a righteous person, a man to be trusted. The world knew nothing but rumors of what Hitler was doing to the Jews of Europe. Oskar, sitting in the heart of the German territories, the confidant of the SS, could tell them. He did, giving the courier his eyewitness account, exaggerating nothing. Then he agreed to travel to Budapest to give Jewish leaders the

60

first full-scale report they would have on the Polish horror.

The Cracow ghetto was nearing its end. The Germans had expanded Plaszow to take in thousands more Jews, and in March 1943 the ghetto was finally closed. The Jews still able to work were marched into Plaszow. The others—the old, sick, unemployable—were shot in their beds or shipped to Auschwitz. For more than seven centuries there had been a Jewish Cracow. Now Cracow was *judenrein*—free of Jews.

Oskar soon learned that Plaszow would be used not only as a forced labor camp but also as a place of execution. Everyone behind the wire was under sentence of death. Today? Tomorrow? It was just a question of when.

Oskar had been assured that his workers living in Plaszow would always arrive on time for their scheduled shifts in his factory. But now all sorts of things held them up. Complaints got him nowhere. So he came up with a bold idea. Why not build a subcamp where his workers could live in his own factory yard? He convinced the Plaszow commander that it made sense. Why not? Oskar could make his Jews work all the harder, and think of the money to be saved; he would feed his Jews at his own expense, and pay for the cost of building the new subcamp. A good fellow, this Schindler, the Nazis said, even if he was infected with that crazy disease of "Jew love!" Besides, Jews from other ghettos to be abolished were to be moved into Plaszow, and Oskar's subcamp would leave room in Plaszow for some of these newcomers.

So up went six new barracks to house 1,200 people. A cookhouse too, and a good shower block, and a laundry. Schindler's Jews knew what they had been given: no SS officer to brutalize them, no guards inside the camp, only at the entrance; a kitchen that supplied more and better soup and bread than in Plaszow. There were long work shifts, yes, but profits had to be made if the factory was to survive. No one died of overwork or hunger or beatings. (Compare it to the forced labor plant run for the giant German chemical firm I.G. Farben, where two out of three died at their labor.) A "paradise," the prisoners thought, a magical paradise that had sprung up here in the midst of hell.

It was not beyond Oskar's daring to contrive a way to photograph the inside workings of Plaszow. He got a written permit from his friend the SS commandant to take two "brother industrialists" on a tour of the "model industrial community." Both men, carrying proper passports, were secret agents of a Jewish rescue organization that wanted visual evidence for the world outside. With Itzhak Stern at his side, Oskar conducted the two men through the camp, as a minicamera captured scene after scene of the killing labor, of the scarred and starving prisoners, of the bloodied wheelbarrows used to transport the dead, and of the mass graves where they lay.

In April 1944, as Oskar reached his thirty-sixth birthday, the Russians rapidly moved west on the offensive. The SS was busy emptying the death camps. They dynamited the gas chambers and crematoria, to leave no recognizable trace. In Plaszow they were burning bodies, thousands of them, immediately after killings. Those buried earlier in the woods were dug up and burned, to remove the evidence of mass murder.

Cracow was alive with rumors. Plaszow would be closed, Oskar learned. Then came an order from the Director of Armaments: Oskar's subcamp would be closed too, and the prisoners would go back into Plaszow, to await "relocation." He knew what that word meant: extermination. The news ripped through his barracks. It's the end, the Jews said. Oskar had given them some safety and sanity. Now they would all die.

Not if Oskar could prevent it. Let me move my factory west to Czechoslovakia, he said to the SS. And let me take my skilled workers with me, along with others in Plaszow whose special talents I could use.

It's all right with me, said SS officer Amon Goeth, smelling out big gifts from Oskar, so long as you get the cooperation you'll need from all the other authorities.

Oskar began preparing a list of people to be moved to wherever the new plant would be. Rumors of the plan reached his workshops. A Schindler list was in the making! Everyone prayed to be on it.

It took rapid maneuvers and handsome bribes to push his plan through. Finally the Berlin bigwigs agreed that Oskar's armaments plant would be moved to an annex of a spinning mill in Brinnlitz, a German village in Moravia, near Oskar's birthplace. Speed was vital; any delays would put his Jewish workers into Auschwitz.

The men on the Schindler list, numbering about 800 (the 300 women were to come on another train), boarded freight cars for Brinnlitz in mid-October 1944. After a hard journey, with long delays en route, they reached Brinnlitz and saw the new labor camp, with watchtowers, wire fence, guard barracks at the gate, and beyond it, the factory and the prisoners' dormitories. There in the courtyard, waiting to greet them, stood Oskar, a splendid sight in his Tyrolean hat, the hat he wore to celebrate his return home to his native mountains.

The new camp had been built at tremendous cost, Oskar's cost. Yet now he had no intention of producing anything useful to the Nazis. Four years earlier, arriving in Cracow, he had meant to get rich. He no longer had any desire to make profits out of slave labor. His personal life had changed too; Emilie, his wife, had come from Zwittau to live with him.

The prisoners quickly sensed that Oskar no longer cared about war production. They worked slowly, and no one speeded them up. The Brinnlitz SS garrison was made up of middle-aged men, reservists called up to replace the younger and more brutal SS men sent to the front lines. They too knew the war was winding down and Germany was losing. They were content to stay out of Oskar's way and not bother his workers.

Then Oskar was arrested again, a third time. The Gestapo handcuffed him and took him back to Cracow. For seven days they grilled him, seeking proof of corruption. But soon his friends in high places stepped in again to vouch for his honesty and loyalty, and on the eighth day they let him go. But while he was in prison, it turned out that Emilie, whom everyone had dismissed as a dull and compliant housewife, had taken over and carried on with Oskar's plans. Not because she was his wife. But because she too cared. She too was committed to human decency.

Oskar was not intimidated by his most recent arrest. His next exploit was to remove from Auschwitz the 300 women who had been on his list in Cracow. They had been slated to go with the other Jews to Brinnlitz. Instead, their train had carried them into Auschwitz. When the car doors opened, the terrified women asked themselves what this meant. Under the floodlights prisoners were sorted out. SS women pointed to them and told the uniformed doctors, These are *Schindlergruppe*. And they were marched off to barracks in the women's camp.

They learned they were marked as a reserve group of "industrial prisoners." Others with that same designation had not been spared, but had disappeared into the killing machine. Weeks passed. The Schindler women, sick, weakened, moved toward death. Some asked, "Where's Schindler now?" Would he keep his promises? But most of them did not despair. In Brinnlitz the men pressed Oskar, "Where are our women?" "I'm getting them out," he answered.

How he succeeded no one is sure. Who had ever heard of anyone being rescued from Auschwitz? The myth already wrapping Oskar's actions in mystery clouded his moves. What seems certain, however, is that Oskar had several telephone conversations with Rudolf Höss, the head of Auschwitz, and two of his chief officers. When the moment seemed ripe, Oskar sent a young woman with a load of liquor, ham, and diamonds to complete a deal with the functionaries. And sometime in November, the *Schindlerfrauen* were called out of their barracks, were showered in a washhouse, had their skulls shaved, and then were marched naked to a quartermaster's hut where they were handed the odds and ends of the clothing of the dead. Half dead themselves, dressed in rags, they were packed tight into the darkness of freight cars. The train rolled out of Auschwitz. In the cold dawn of the next day they were ordered out at a rural siding. Shivering, coughing, they stumbled ahead to a large gate guarded by SS men. Behind the gate rose tall brick chimneys. Panic seized them: Was this another death factory? But as they reached the gate, they could see Oskar standing in the midst of the SS men. He stepped forward to greet the women. "You have nothing more to worry about," he said. "You're with me now." One of them remembered years later that on seeing him she felt that "he was our father, he was our mother, he was our only faith. He never let us down."

Oskar wandered all over Moravia, buying food for his Jews, and arms and ammunition so they could defend themselves in case the SS tried to kill them during a retreat. His factory still produced nothing. Or almost nothing. They did ship one truckload of antitank shells so badly made that they were returned because they failed quality control tests. Good, said Oskar when an official complaint was made, now I know nobody has been killed by my product.

How did his factory pass inspection? For there were plenty of inspectors sent in routinely. Just as routinely, Oskar dined them and liquored them up so richly they scarcely knew what they were looking at in his workshops. And off they went, loaded with gifts of cigarettes and cognac. Some said he bought shells from other Czech factories and passed them off as his own if an inspector really tried to look at something. Whatever Oskar's confidence tricks were, they worked.

Then on May 7, 1945, the prisoners heard BBC radio broadcast the news of the German surrender. The war in Europe would end at midnight on May 8th. Oskar already knew the Russians were about to enter Brinnlitz. Somehow he had to avoid them and reach the Americans, where he might hope for better treatment. But first, with the SS guards present, he spoke to the prisoners. He invited the SS to leave, and asked the prisoners to let them go. The

SS men dropped their weapons at the gate, and by midnight all had gone.

Next, Oskar and Emilie prepared to leave. They put on prisoner's stripes, and eight Jews volunteered to travel with them, to protect these two Germans from anyone who might try to harm them. They carried with them a letter attesting to the record of the Schindlers' good deeds all these years.

It was hard for the other prisoners to say good-bye. They handed Oskar a gift. It was a ring made of gold donated from the bridgework of a Jewish prisoner. On it they had inscribed this Talmudic verse: "Whoever saves a single soul, it is as if he had saved the whole world."

On the road they ran into an American infantry battalion, which included several Jewish soldiers and a field rabbi. When the Americans heard the Schindler story from the Jews, they embraced Oskar. He was safe.

Everything Oskar had owned was confiscated by the Russians. He was penniless. But his "family"—the *Schindlerjuden* (Schindler's Jews), as they proudly called themselves—would care for him the rest of his life. He and Emilie took up farming in Argentina for ten years, then went back to Germany. Oskar never prospered again. He became more dependent on the survivors, who gave him financial and emotional support.

In 1961 he visited Israel as a guest of the *Schindlerjuden*, and was welcomed ecstatically by the public and the press. "We do not forget the sorrows of Egypt, we do not forget Haman, we do not forget Hitler. Among the unjust, we do not forget the just. Remember Oskar Schindler."

In 1974 he died in Germany. At his request, he was buried in the Latin Cemetery in Jerusalem.

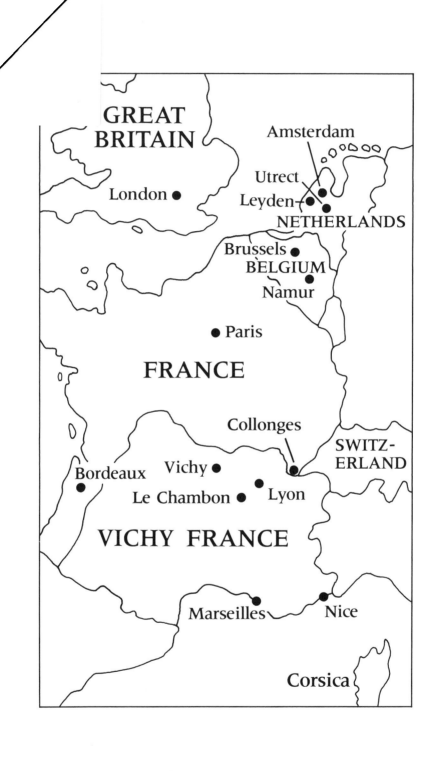

6 The Miracle of Le Chambon

From Poland and Oskar Schindler we turn to the opposite side of Europe. To France and another remarkable man, André Trocmé. Schindler and Trocmé: two men who could not have been more different in origin, upbringing, temperament, occupation, habits. In almost nothing were they alike, except their caring and the will to help.

But before we tell the story of André Trocmé and the people of his village, Le Chambon, let's look at France after the Germans conquered it in the spring of 1940. At the time of her defeat France held 350,000 Jews. Almost half were Jews whose ancestors had lived there for centuries. The others were recent refugees from other parts of Europe the Nazis had overrun. When France collapsed, about two thirds of the Jews fled to southern France to avoid the invading Germans. The others remained mostly in Paris.

A new French government that would collaborate with the Nazis was set up under the aged Marshal Pétain in the south, at Vichy. In the north the German military and the Gestapo ruled directly. Thousands of the Jews who had sought refuge in the unoccupied south managed to flee abroad. Many were helped by the Portuguese Consul-General at Bordeaux, Aristedes de Sousa Mendes. Nearly 100,000 Jews were in his area, close to the Spanish-French border, and all had but one desire—to escape to Spain across the Pyrenees and into Portugal, a neutral country. But the Portuguese government refused to grant entry visas to any refugees, especially to Jews.

The Portuguese consul, Mendes, was a lawyer and a devout Catholic. He could not close his eyes to the refugees' torment. He took a great many Jews into his own home. Thousands of others lined up outside, hoping the visa policy would change. The consul came out and spoke to them. My government has denied you visas, he said, and I cannot let you die. Our constitution says that the religious and political views of a foreigner are not grounds of refusal of asylum in Portugal. I have decided to act on the spirit of this principle. I shall give anyone who desires a visa. Even if I am dismissed from my post I cannot but act as a Christian, faithful to the dictates of my conscience.

With his family to help him, Mendes sat down in front of his house and for three days stamped visas for thousands of Jews. His government learned of this at once and in a rage ordered him back to Portugal. On his way there he passed through the French town of Bayonne and saw refugees there waiting outside the Portuguese consulate. Outranking the Portuguese official in Bayonne, Mendes took over and stamped visas all day long. Later, at the French border town of Hendaye, he found Jews holding visas he had stamped but still unable to cross into Spain because the border was closed by agreement with Portugal. He instructed the Jews to move to a nearby border station, where no order had been given to bar refugees, and there they crossed into Spain and safety.

Mendes saved the lives of more than 10,000 Jews. Yet for defying orders, his government stripped him of his post and his right to practice law, and blacklisted him from other jobs. Though he had a family of twelve children, Mendes said afterward that he had no regrets; he was proud of what he did: "If thousands of Jews can suffer because of one Catholic [he meant Hitler], then surely it is permitted for one Catholic to suffer for so many Jews. I could not act otherwise. I accept everything that has befallen me with love."

Mendes died in poverty in 1954.

What happened to the Jews in France is an example of the choices that confronted regimes in countries occupied by the Germans. The Germans could not carry out everything they wanted to do by themselves. Even the most brutal conquerors need local assistance. In the south of France the Germans let Pétain hold the reins. His government had two options: to join the Germans in persecuting the Jews or to protect the Jews and resist their deportation.

The choice of the Vichy government was soon clear. Within months of the surrender to the Germans in 1940 it adopted racist laws that were in some ways harsher than Germany's. When the Nazis demanded the deportation of the Jews from France, 35,000 French militia and police carried it out, with only 2,500 Gestapo involved. About 75,000 Jews—a quarter of the community—were forced onto cattle cars bound for the death camps in the east. Only 2,500, or 3 percent, came back.

What shaped such decisions was the character of the regime, its relationship to Germany, and its assumptions about the outcome of the war. No less important was the force of anti-Semitism among its own people. Vichy's actions reflected popular feeling against the Jews. Anti-Semitism had been as strong in France as in Germany or Russia. Now it was even stronger against foreign Jewish refugees, but it affected French-born Jews too. In Paris in July 1942 the first mass arrests of Jews, including women and children, took place. The next month the Germans demanded 50,000 Jews from the southern zone. The Vichy government zealously complied. It even went beyond the order—which was confined to adults for the time being—and proposed sending the children as well.

Many Jewish families in the south left their children behind, thousands of whom were held in detention camps. Still, over 6,000 children in that year alone were sent to Auschwitz from France. (All told, 17,000 children under the age of seventeen were deported from France.)

The deportations were renewed in 1943, and again the French police took charge of massive roundups in both the north and south. Thousands tried to flee the country. But Spain and Switzerland, which shared borders with France, discouraged refugees and turned many back. A desperate traffic began along these borders. Local guides took people across, risking capture by police and border guards. Big sums were demanded by some profiteers for passage to safety; often the Jews were robbed on the journey, or shaken down by people posing as police.

When Jews could not escape abroad, they tried to go underground. Some found shelter in homes and religious sanctuaries. In the town of Roanne, for instance, one-third of the local Jews were hidden by non-Jews. Children had the best chance of survival in hiding. The very young might be taken by foster mothers in remote country districts. The Catholics took many children into nunneries. They were given new names and papers to conceal their Jewish identity. (Their real names were, when possible, recorded in secret by Jewish social agencies.)

Many people joined in the effort to rescue Jewish children. They were Catholics, Protestants, and both leftists and rightists. Some acted alone, some in small groups, some with the help of organizations, both Jewish and non-Jewish. American organizations such as the Quakers, the Unitarians, and the YWCA fought hard with the Vichy regime to win authorization to take Jewish children out of the detention camps.

What was it like for parents to give up children in the frail hope of saving them? And with the knowledge they might never see them again? It took great courage, and some were unable to part from their younger children. The teenagers didn't want to leave their parents, thinking it cowardly to escape the fate of the family. But separation did occur, and many children were taken to houses in the country, peaceful places where they might be protected until the war's end. In one country manor, for example, about one hundred children from ages four to sixteen were housed. However, when the Germans occupied southern France in late 1942, it became very dangerous to keep Jewish children in such large groups. With the help of rescue groups linked to one another as well as to the Resistance networks, the homes were gradually closed and the children placed in hiding.

The children were "aryanized" first—given new names, identity papers, ration cards—before they were taken to non-Jewish homes in places where nobody knew who they really were except perhaps for one trusted person. A child had to be convinced she was no longer "Frieda" this but "Françoise" that, and to stick to her new name no matter what. A woman who worked with the children recalled:

One day I was so upset about a little boy who had already changed his name once before, in order to make it sound less Polish-Jewish and more French-Jewish, and now had to change it again, to make it sound more French-Christian. To comfort me, he said, "Don't worry, I'm getting used to new names." Then all of a sudden he mused, "Maybe nobody remembers my real name."

When the French rounded up 13,000 stateless Jews in Paris on July 16, 1942, it was Marie Chotel, a Catholic concierge, and her husband Henri who saved a little Jewish girl's life. Odette Meyer, age seven, was the daughter of Polish Jews who had lived in France for many years. When the police came that morning to search the apartment house for Jews, Madame Marie was called and held the police off with faked anti-Semitic chatter and lots of wine while Odette and her mother hid in a broom closet. The police never got around to searching their room.

Madame Marie's husband, Henri, a member of the underground, was called from his job and came at once to escort Odette to safety. Years later Odette recalls what happened:

We walked outside. There were German soldiers everywhere. He held my hand. I was trembling. My hand was shaking. I remember that there were trucks full of

74

Jews being rounded up, and he told me, "Remember, look at your feet and keep walking. If anyone calls you, don't answer. Don't look up. Don't answer." So we walked like that. Nobody called. And I looked at my feet as we walked. We reached the subway entrance, and I remember a wonderful sense of safety as we went down into the subway. The station was almost deserted, and we had to wait for a train to take us to the railway station. There we met with other children, and a Gentile woman who was to accompany us to our hiding place in the country. It was prearranged by the Resistance and the Catholics in the Resistance. I ended up in a Catholic village for the duration of the occupation. If I had not been saved by this man and woman I know precisely what my fate would have been. I would have ended up in the gas chamber at Birkenau.

Ninety-five percent of the Jewish children in Paris were taken that day; only five percent were saved.

Why did Madame Marie help? She was born to an unwed mother in a village in Lorraine. With little education, she went to work at an early age, first as a chambermaid, then as a waitress, and finally as a concierge in Paris. A plump, pleasant, down-to-earth woman, she rarely went to church but lived a good life. Childless, she declared when Odette was born that she would be her godmother. She never allowed anti-Semitic neighbors to abuse Odette's family. Odette remembers her this way:

Madame Marie had a very simple philosophy. We were Jewish and she did not want to impose her religion on us, but she told me a story: "The heart is like an apart-

75

ment, and if it's messy and there is nothing to offer, no food or drink to offer guests, nobody will want to come. But if it's clean and dusted every day, and if it's pretty and there are flowers and food and drink for guests, people will want to come and they will want to stay for dinner. And if it's super nice, God himself will want to come." That was it.

Madame Marie was so important to little Odette that even the sound of her name was comforting. When Odette was hiding in the village and passing as a Catholic, it was strange and scary. But when she found out that the peasants affectionately called the Virgin Mary "Madame Marie," she knew she would be all right. She thought, "If they have a Madame Marie here, then I'm safe!"

One more story of a helping hand before we move on to André Trocmé and Le Chambon. John Weidner was raised in a Christian family that believed love was the aim of their lives. He knew from the Bible that Jesus Christ, who was himself a Jew, had said that the greatest commandment was "to love our neighbors as ourselves." At home and at school he was taught to be compassionate and to serve others. His father, a Seventh-Day Adventist minister, taught Latin and Greek in the school John attended.

John was working in Paris when the Germans invaded France. He had read Hitler's *Mein Kampf* and knew how the Jews were persecuted in Germany. But when the Nazis began to arrest Jews in France, he couldn't believe what he saw happening—"the inhumanity of man against man."

I remember being in the railroad station at Lyons where I saw a group of Jewish women and children who had been arrested and were being deported to the east. One woman had a baby in her arms. The baby started to cry and make a lot of noise in the railroad station. The SS officer who was in charge ordered the woman to make the baby stop crying, but she could not do it. In a rage, the officer took the baby out of the arms of the woman, smashed the baby on the floor, and crushed its head. We heard the wail of that mother. It was something terrible. And all the while, the SS officers stood around laughing.

Such horrors violated everything John believed in, and he resolved to help the Jews. Since he knew the French-Swiss border region around Collonges, where he had gone to school, he went there to help Jews cross into neutral Switzerland. At first he did it alone, then family and friends joined him, but there was so much to be done, he needed more help. So with others he organized a network called "Dutch-Paris" and set up a route to bring people from Holland to Belgium to France and then across the border to Geneva. During the war they passed more than 1,000 people, mostly Jews and some Allied airmen too, through that route.

It was hard and dangerous. One of their agents was arrested and could not hold up under torture. She gave the names of all those in the group she knew, and in one day half their 300 members were captured and deported to Nazi camps. Forty, including John's sister Gabrielle, never came back. John himself was taken by the Gestapo, beaten, and tortured, but was able to escape.

What he remembers most about the Nazis is their voices—hard, brutal. They had no humanity. They were force and violence incarnate. His happier memories are of "the simple, good people who were ready to risk all, to help, to give shelter." He saw it in people of all religions or of no religion. "It taught me that you can have all kinds of theories and all kinds of creeds, but if you do not have love in action, those theories and those creeds do not mean anything at all."

Now to Le Chambon. It is a village in south central France, in the hills above Lyons. Here the winters are long and cold, and the village is often snowed in. Less than 1 percent of the nation is Protestant, but this village, with 3,000 souls, is Protestant and has been since the 1500s. Most of its people are descendants of the Huguenots who fled to this high plateau so they could continue practicing their own kind of Christianity without punishment. For many generations its pastors and people suffered persecution for their faith; some of them were hanged or burned for it. Resisting persecution gave the villagers a close-knit solidarity that has never been broken. That unity and devotion made possible the rescue of thousands of Jewish children and adults in World War II.

Pastor André Trocmé, his wife Magda, and their four children were living in the village when the war broke out. They were a couple of mixed origins. André's mother was German and his father French; Magda's father was Italian and her mother Russian. The young pastor André Trocmé had been called to the mountain community in 1934. He found the old Huguenot spirit alive there. "The humblest peasant home has its Bible," he wrote, "and the father reads it every day. So these people, who do not read the papers but the scriptures, do not stand on the moving soil of opinion but on the rock of the Word of the Lord."

Trocmé, nearing forty when the war reached France, was a tall man with fair skin, blue eyes, and immense energy. He was given to deep affection as well as to powerful anger at injustice. His wife, of the same age, matched him in energy and devotion to anyone who needed food or shelter.

Soon after the Trocmés came to Le Chambon, he and Éduoard Theis, a close friend and half-time minister under Trocmé, started the Cévenol School. Both men had joined the international pacifist organization called the Fellowship of Reconciliation while studying in Paris, and had worked with the labor unions and the poor. Theis, a powerfully built man, was a bit older than André. He and his wife Mildred and their eight daughters shared the same commitment as the Trocmés to obeying the Sermon on the Mount. Their small private school prepared teenagers for entrance to the universities. Its creed was nonviolence, in the spirit of internationalism and peace. Both Trocmé and Theis were conscientious objectors, not a popular cause in that time.

As Hitler seized more and more of Europe, the Cévenol School expanded rapidly, taking in the children of refugees from central and eastern Europe. The students, faculty, and classrooms soon spread all over the village. From the pulpit as well as in the school, Trocmé and Theis preached resistance to evil and preparation for any opportunity to do something in the spirit of nonviolent resistance.

The two pastors did not believe that nonviolence means one should be passive or inactive. Resistance to violence, to war, to Nazism, to evil, means preparing and organizing for *action* against them. But to believe in the preciousness of human life also makes it impossible to justify killing.

Le Chambon was in the unoccupied zone. One day the order came to Cévenol to place a picture of Marshal Pétain on the school wall. They did not do it. Then came an order to begin each school day by raising the flag. They did not do it. Then an order to give the Fascist salute to the flag. They did not do it. The villagers noticed Cévenol's quiet acts of resistance; it was one way of saying no to tyranny.

Pétain had established youth camps in France and ordered all young men when they reached the age of twenty to spend eight months in one, to be trained, like the Hitler youth, in Nazi beliefs and practices. The youth of Le Chambon never went to these camps. So Georges Lamirand, Vichy's Minister of Youth, came to Le Chambon to encourage the youth to, as Trocmé saw it, give up their consciences. During his visit, a dozen Cévenol students handed Lamirand a formal protest against the recent deportation of the Jews of Paris.

They warned the Vichy government:

We feel obliged to tell you that there are among us a certain number of Jews. But we make no distinction between Jews and non-Jews. It is contrary to the Gospel teaching. If our comrades, whose only fault is to be born in another religion, received the orders to let themselves be deported, or even examined, they would disobey the orders received, and we would try to hide them as best we could.

The people of Le Chambon had publicly declared themselves. The district police chief was furious, and blamed Trocmé for the confrontation. This "deportation," he said, was only a "regrouping" in Poland of the European Jews. Then he let it slip that the Vichy government had ordered him to take the Jews from Le Chambon. At this time knowledge of the death camps had not yet reached Le Chambon. But what the people did know, said Trocmé, was that "it is evil to deliver a brother who has entrusted himself to us. That we would not consent to."

The two pastors and their students planned at once how to hide the Jews living in the village, or those who might come. Concealing refugees was no novelty to them. They knew the hideouts the Huguenots had used 300 years before. They alerted the whole countryside; no farmer would refuse to hide Jews when the time came.

Two weeks later, on a Saturday night, two khaki police vans drove into the village square under motorcycle escort. The police summoned Trocmé. You know all the Jews in this place, they said. Give us a list. Trocmé replied truthfully that he did not know their names. (They all had false identity cards, and he had avoided learning their true names.) But, he continued, even if I had such a list, I wouldn't give it to you. These people came here seeking shelter. I am their pastor, their shepherd. I will not betray them.

If you don't obey my order by tomorrow night, the police chief threatened, you yourself will be arrested and deported. Resistance is useless. We know where your Jews are hiding.

When the police went to sleep in their buses, Trocmé went to his office and met with the Boy Scouts and his

81

Bible class leaders. He sent them to outlying farms and to village houses that had been concealing refugees to warn the Jews to leave and hide in the woods for a while. It had all been prearranged.

The next morning the police searched every house in the village and most of the nearby farms. No Jew was found. For three weeks they returned again and again to comb the houses from cellar to attic. Not a single arrest could be made. At last they left.

A strange thing began to happen. As Le Chambon strengthened its resistance, many of the Vichy police began to help the villagers and their Jews. Not officially, but personally, some became converted by the living example of people who would not hate or harm the innocent. More and more often orders to catch people who had done no wrong were quietly ignored. Even after the Germans came down to occupy southern France and the Gestapo took charge of the police, the Trocmés would get mysterious phone calls in the night: "Attention! Attention! Tomorrow morning!" And at these warnings the Jews would disappear.

The beginnings of all this go back to the winter of 1940–1941, after the fall of France. One bitter night Magda Trocmé heard a knock at the door. She opened it to find a woman shrouded in snow, trembling with cold and fear. She was a German Jew, she said. "Come in, come in," said Magda. The woman had fled Germany, lived some time in the occupied zone, and when persecution got worse, slipped into the Vichy zone. She was in danger, she said, and had heard that in Le Chambon someone might help her. Magda calmed the woman, fed her, and made her comfortable, then went for help. She knew the woman had to get false identity papers quickly, for there were frequent surprise checks that might lead to her deportation back into Hitler's hands. Helping refugees was never an easy thing to do. But the Trocmés and Le Chambon were beginning to learn how to make their village the safest place in Europe for Jews.

After this encounter with their first refugee, André's church council gave him permission to find ways to help the refugees pouring into southern France, and promised him supplies and money. He went to talk with the American Quakers at their office in Marseilles; he knew the Quakers were doing much for the inmates of the terrible internment camps in southern France. He talked with the Quaker Burns Chalmers, who had long known of Trocmé's great influence as a nonviolent leader in his region. The two men agreed that the best way to help was to make Le Chambon a refuge for children. They wanted the children of refugees to know there were people outside their own families, strangers, who cared for them. By easing the suffering of these children they could give them hope and reasons to live moral lives of their own.

The Quakers did all they could to prevent the refugees in the camps from being sent to forced labor in Germany or, later, to the death camps. But if, nevertheless, the parents were deported, the Quakers took charge of the children and agreed to house them outside the camp. It was very hard to find a community that would risk its own safety to take in such dangerous guests. It meant boarding them, feeding them, educating them, protecting them.

How many villages had leaders willing to put their own

lives—and even the very existence of their communities—at risk? Like most people, they were too concerned with their own security to make such a commitment. And to take strangers, foreigners, Jews, into the intimate daily lives of their homes?

But Trocmé said we'll do it. And Le Chambon began its work.

At the heart of the rescue effort were André Trocmé and his church. Every Sunday in their church, Trocmé and Theis delivered sermons that strengthened the villagers' resolve. Their favorite Bible passages were the Good Samaritan Story in Luke and the Sermon on the Mount. They talked of the need to obey one's conscience, even when it conflicted with the orders of the state. The greatest obligation is to help the weak, even if it means disobedience to the strong. Once, in a sermon after the roundup of the Jews in Paris, André said, "It is humiliating to Europe that such things can happen, and that we the French cannot act against such barbaric deeds that come from a time we once believed was past. The Christian Church should drop to its knees and beg pardon of God for its present incapacity and cowardice."

More and more refugees came to Le Chambon. A national leader of Trocmé's Reformed Church tried to make André stop the work. He charged it was endangering the existence not only of the village but of the Protestant Church in France. André replied, "If we stop, many of them will starve to death, or die of exposure, or be deported and killed. We cannot stop." André then offered his resignation to the village church council. They flatly refused it, encouraging him to go on helping Jews, no matter what orders or laws he violated in doing it.

Of great help to André were the leaders of the thirteen youth groups he had formed in the church to study the Bible. He met with these leaders once every two weeks to discuss a Bible passage they had been thinking about. Then the leaders went to their thirteen groups to talk with them about the chosen passages. So stimulating were the groups that they grew bigger and bigger. Their leaders became the communications network for sheltering the Jews. Out of their sessions came practical plans for "overcoming evil with good." The "responsibles," these leaders were called, and they fulfilled their mission fervently.

But it was the Le Chambon villagers who made everything possible. They made the plans work. For the refugees the village houses were the heart of their life in hiding. Some of the houses were funded by organizations abroad, by Catholic groups, the World Council of Churches, governments such as Sweden or Switzerland. One group, the Cimade, started and led only by women, developed teams to conduct Jews through the mountains into Switzerland.

There were also boarding houses, pensions, near the center of the village that helped. Madame Eyraud's took only boys—hundreds of them during the war, many of them Jews whom she cleverly disguised or hid when surprise raids came. Another family, the Marions, sheltered only adolescent girls, many of them Jewish students at the Cévenol School. There were a dozen or more such boarding houses in the village, and a much greater number of private homes that took in children and families. Sometimes for a short stay, sometimes for years.

In the course of the Nazi occupation about 2,500 Jewish refugees of all ages came to Le Chambon. After Magda

85

Trocmé opened her door to the first refugee, no one in the village ever turned one away or ever betrayed one. All the refugees made themselves useful: They cooked, they cleaned, they washed clothes, they sewed, they repaired furniture, they tended the sick, they watched over children, they did every kind of task possible, no matter what the length of their stay.

When the villagers agreed to make Le Chambon a sanctuary for refugees, André asked his young second cousin, Daniel Trocmé, to head two of the first funded houses. One was called the Crickets, the other the House of the Rocks. Daniel, a teacher, was in charge of children whose parents had been deported. Slender and intense, with a heart ailment that was only worsened by the mountain altitude, he worked devotedly for the children. He made their soup, repaired their shoes, patched their clothes, taught their lessons.

In the summer of 1943 a police agent was shot in Le Chambon by the Resistance. Angered by the killing, the Gestapo rounded up all the young Jews in Daniel's care and deported them to the killing camp at Maidanek in Poland. Some Jewish children survived and reported that Daniel had been gassed and incinerated. It was the Gestapo's only successful raid on Le Chambon.

Earlier that year André, Theis, and a teacher were arrested and sent to a detention camp in Gurs. Death, they thought, was next. But powerful influence seems to have secured their release in a month. Now, after the raid that took Daniel and the children, both pastors learned they were on a Gestapo death list. They disappeared. Trocmé hid in the mountains for a year but stayed in touch with his people. Theis joined the Cimade group and helped take refugees through the mountains of Switzerland.

In June 1944 the Allies landed in Normandy. Soon after, Trocmé returned to his village. He found many of the young men in the Cévenol School had joined the Resistance, giving up nonviolence to commit sabotage and to ambush German troops. But Le Chambon had become an even busier station on the underground railroad carrying refugees to safety. The houses for the children were always full. Magda and the other women had gone on with the work, keeping the village a place where conscience prevailed.

In September 1944 French troops liberated Le Chambon. The refugees left, the children's houses closed, and the number of the school's students dropped by half. The villagers felt relief, and joy. André, now forty-three years old, was worn down by the long struggle to save lives. These, he knew, had been the harshest—but the most useful—years of his life. A few years later he became the European head of the Fellowship of Reconciliation. He died in 1971. That "dangerous, difficult Trocmé," as he had been called by his national church, had made goodness happen in Le Chambon.

7 A Nation of Rescuers

In the village of Le Chambon all the people came together to save the lives of thousands of Jews. In the country of Denmark another spectacular act of human solidarity took place. Danish Jewry was saved by the action of a whole nation. How did that happen?

Fewer than 8,000 Jews lived in Denmark when the war began, and most of them in the capital city of Copenhagen. Only 0.2 percent of the population of 4.5 million, Jews had been absorbed into the country's economic and cultural life. Many had intermarried with Christians. They had enjoyed the full rights of citizenship for over 125 years. Anti-Semitism was almost unknown. When Hitler began his assault upon the German Jews in the early 1930s, it deeply offended the Danes. The few Nazi sympathizers in Denmark were a despised minority.

In April 1940 the Germans made a lightning attack upon Denmark. The Danish people were taken completely by surprise, and the tiny Danish army was quickly overpowered. The government agreed to surrender. But it insisted on certain conditions. Since the Nazis considered the Danes a "Nordic" people like themselves, they didn't expect much trouble from them. So why not make a concession or two?

The Danish conditions included no discrimination against Jews, and no Danish forces to support the German army. The Jews are Danes like all other citizens, the government said, and must not be separated from the rest of our people.

In losing their freedom the Danes felt terrible anger and shame. But so long as 8,000 Jews lived freely in Denmark, the people told themselves that they had not been conquered, in spite of the presence of German troops in their streets. The Danish Jews became a symbol of national integrity. A resistance movement sprang up in the hope of preserving national independence and democratic values. While most Danes chose passive resistance, many others armed themselves for active resistance and used sabotage, riots, and strikes against the Nazi occupation.

Angered by the acts of resistance, early in 1943 the Nazis tried to push the Danish government to adopt anti-Jewish measures. The government refused, for to defend the Jews was to defend Denmark's own struggle for survival. Then the Germans ordered the government to ghettoize the Jews and make them wear yellow stars. The king, Christian X, resisted, supported by his entire people, whose inner strength was added to by news of the defeats the "invincible" Germans had suffered at Stalingrad and in Africa. And now the Allies had landed in Italy and the Mussolini regime had fallen.

In August 1943 strikes and sabotage reached a new peak in Denmark. The Germans declared martial law and took direct control of the government. Hitler's "experts" on the "final solution" arrived to plan the deportation to the death camps.

October 1 was the date the Germans chose for the mass arrest of the Jews. The plot was prepared in complete secrecy. Georg Duckwitz, the German shipping attaché in Copenhagen, received secret instructions to prepare four cargo ships to transport all the Jews at one time. Duckwitz ignored the great personal risk to himself and told two Danish political leaders of the imminent danger to the Jews. They passed the word to the head of Copenhagen's Jewish community, who found it hard to believe.

The news was given in the synagogue on September 29, the eve of the Jewish New Year. The Jews at worship scattered throughout the city to warn every Jew they could reach to hide or flee. Danish underground workers carried the alarm to still others in the city and to Jews living beyond. Everywhere people in the streets were stopped and queried: Are you Jewish? Do you have Jewish friends or neighbors? Tell them! Danish homes were opened to Jews as temporary hiding places while rescue plans were shaped.

For the Jewish citizens the warning to flee came as a violent shock. The Germans in Denmark had not succeeded with any of the preliminary steps against the Jews that they had carried out everywhere else. Up until this moment the Danish Jews had led quite normal lives. They wore no yellow badges, they lived in no ghettos, they still had all their property, and they were not going hungry. They felt about as anxious for their future as other Danes, no more. So when the crisis came they were stunned. At first they could not believe the warning. They had not organized a plan for acting in such a crisis. Happily, however, body and spirit were still intact; there had been no persecution to destroy them.

When rumors of the deportation flew through Denmark, Jews began to run at once. Most thought only to hide for a brief while, until the storm blew over, and then to return home. Others feared the worst and wanted to escape to Sweden. All relied only on families and friends for help. Their own community had failed to prepare any group rescue plan, which is why the few hundred taken by the Nazis were mostly the old and the poor, trapped in the institutions that cared for them.

As soon as the Swedish government heard of the deportation plan, it told Berlin that it was ready to transfer all Danish Jews to its own neutral territory. The Germans were not interested. They did not want simply to get Jews out of Denmark. They wanted to kill them. And quickly. The only way the Jews could escape was to cross the narrow passage of water between Denmark and Sweden. The Germans knew that, of course, and placed their gunboats along the seacoast to make sure no Jews would get away. German police cars patrolled the streets while the Gestapo and soldiers guarded all ports.

Between the warning on September 29 and the zero hour on October 1 there were only two days to act. Unless a great many Danes were ready to risk their lives to help, it would not be possible to rescue thousands.

On Friday night, October 1, with the cutting of all telephone connections, the German action began. The Danish writer Erling Foss tells what happened:

Everywhere where there were doorplates with Jewish names, the German police troops appeared. In villa quarters they surrounded the houses. They did not take the sick and even released those who could prove they were half-Jews. Also those who were married to non-Jews were released. The expression in the eyes of people brought aboard the two ships was heartrending, according to reports from town. . . .

From the various assembly points police vans proceeded to take up their position at certain spots, from where the arresting columns were sent out. At the same time the telephone services were completely suspended, so completely that even the flight service and "emergency" were not functioning. Ritzau's Bureau [the official Danish news agency] was occupied to insure that the teleprinter was not used. . . . The roundup was carried out in various ways—it is difficult to give a clear picture. Some patrols were content merely to ring and to go away again if the door was not opened. Elsewhere, and this occurred often, they smashed in the door and woke up the whole house to cross-examine people in the other apartments as to the whereabouts of the Jews. . . . Danish-speaking people accompanied each patrol. The most frightful scenes were played out, with whole families being dragged away, and these produced anger among the population deeper and more heartfelt than that aroused by any previous action. People as old as ninety-two and babies two months old were seized and put on board ship. Mrs. Texière, the 102-year-old mother of the actor Jakob Texière, was among those deported.

The old-age home next to the synagogue in Krystalgade was surrounded by 150 men, and all the inmates, aged from sixty to ninety, were taken away. The Germans behaved here with incredible brutality. They burst into the room of an old lady who was paralyzed and had been bedridden for eleven years, and since she could not get up they bound her with leather straps and dragged her to the synagogue, where all the old people were assembled. Here they were cross-examined as to their acquaintance with this or that saboteur, and since it was only natural that they did not know any, they were beaten and kicked. From the synagogue, as from all the rooms, the Germans stole any valuables they could lay their hands on; and the German police troops relieved themselves in the synagogue.

Nazi records show that 284 Jews were seized on that night. The low number made the German action a failure. The Jews had evaded their grasp and disappeared overnight. If the Nazis were capable of learning a lesson, it would have been that the "final solution" could not be carried out when the people among whom the Jews lived opposed it.

How did the Danes do it? Flight to Sweden was never an easy thing. For years resistance fighters marked for Nazi vengeance and some Jews had tried to escape by that route. German minefields and patrol boats made such illegal crossings very risky. Some made it; some failed. When it seemed that the Germans were invincible, the Swedes were not too eager to help; they feared that taking in refugees would endanger their neutral position.

The threat to deport the Jews aroused the Danes more than anything else the Germans had done. It was an order that had no military or economic motive: only the aim of total destruction of an innocent people. The Germans never expected this one act would transform what had been largely a passive resistance into an open struggle.

They had turned the peaceful, law-abiding Danes into underground fighters.

On October 3, the bishops of Denmark issued a letter of protest against the deportation, declaring that to persecute Jews was irreconcilable with the Christian instruction to love thy neighbor. The church guaranteed to "our Jewish brothers and sisters the same freedom we ourselves treasure more than life itself." To help rescue the Jews was to defend right and freedom for all. Danes would not obey the orders of any authority if asked to perform a deed contrary to their consciences.

The rescue effort was a herculean task to undertake almost overnight. It meant warning the Jews, finding hiding places for them, raising the funds, and lining up boats to transfer them to Sweden. Jews were warned by friends, neighbors, trade unionists, teachers, employers, students, journalists, politicians, ministers, civil servants—even a few Germans. Most of the Jews got word from several sources, and many times over. Within a few hours Jews arranged to transfer to friends and associates their homes, businesses, valuables, bank accounts, and whatever else, and were ready to flee.

But where to? Some moved to a friend's house or summer home. People everywhere took in whole families, provided beds, food, and clothing. Payment was refused. Even complete strangers would offer the key to their home to Jews they met on the street.

The hardest task was to find the Jews who had fled the city to hide in the woods or elsewhere. Most of these were working people, without the money to escape to Sweden. Members of the medical profession took over the search for them, found them, got them back to the city, and hid them in hospitals until they could transfer them to Sweden. They thought it a natural task for their profession to protect and preserve life.

It took many fishermen—willing to risk their lives and their boats—to carry out the rescue operations. All kinds of boats were used. Some could carry only a few refugees, others a larger number. Cargo boats whose holds could conceal hundreds of people and regular passenger vessels scheduled to sail to German ports would hide Jews in their holds, go a bit off course, meet a Swedish boat by prearrangement, and transfer the refugees.

Most of the rescue organizers worked directly with fishermen. But Erling Kiaer, a bookbinder with little experience at sea, bought his own small boat and ran an escape route across the narrowest point between Denmark and Sweden. His rescue group collected Jews who were hiding in private houses in the coastal villages and sailed them across the straits to Sweden.

A Jewish woman tells how her perilous rescue was carried out:

A man came and gave the signal to start. We were taken by taxi to the beach near a little fishing harbor. Each of the four passengers and the organizer were then hidden under a bush by the shore. The plan was that at a certain time we were to crawl along the beach to the harbor, where there was a watchtower manned by Germans. We lay a whole day waiting for darkness. Up on the road we could hear cars drive by and we shivered with fright. Once a truck stopped right opposite our hiding place, but luckily it contained underground fighters who comforted us with the news that there were armed resistance fighters in the nearby ditches. As far as we knew, the Germans in the watchtower had been bribed to turn a blind eye. At seven o'clock in the evening, a strange sight revealed itself. From the bushes along the beach human forms crawled out on their stomachs. We discovered that these were other passengers of whose presence we had been completely unaware. After a while we reached the fishing boat without mishap and were herded into the hold, like herrings in a barrel. As there was not enough space down below, a few passengers were wrapped in fishing nets and in sacks on the deck.

Owing to mines, a considerable detour had to be made and there was also a danger of running aground—soundings had to be constantly taken. The fishermen had been informed that we would pass by two German patrol boats, equipped with searchlights. We had a crew of two and twenty-one refugees, who in fact did not see one another until next day. At eight o'clock the boat sailed after we had said goodbye to our various helpers, among whom was a well-known freedom fighter, whose name or cover name we did not know—all we knew was that he was probably a schoolteacher, and later in Sweden we heard that he had been killed by the Germans. Shortly after our sailing, a wind blew up and many became seasick and were forced to come up on deck and retch, as they could not bear to be in the smelly hold.

Then we saw the searchlight of the German patrol boat. The engine was immediately stopped and we were ordered to stand stiff and still around the wheelhouse, whose weak light could have given us away. We made our way slowly and with as little noise as possible. Everyone thought his last hour had come and was ready to jump overboard and drown, rather than be taken by the Germans. Dramatic scenes took place—someone lit a lamp on the masthead and the others trembled with rage, quarrels broke out, nervousness spread and actually, we could very easily have been discovered. Tension on board was extreme, though we were happy that freedom and rescue lay before us on the horizon. However, the passengers calmed down after the initial danger had passed and made every effort to stay calm, though every muscle was tense for fear of discovery.

The little boat had in the meantime gone off course because of the gale, and twenty-one lives lay in the hands of two fishermen. Gradually it began to grow light, but we had no idea of the boat's position. Would we land on Bornholm? Would we ever be saved? At seven in the morning, land was sighted, but what land? Dared we hope that it was the Swedish coast—our goal was Trelleborg. The boat approached the coast; we hoped that liberty was at hand. We were really in Swedish territorial waters. The Danish flag was raised and people threw their arms around one another and cried for joy. We were saved at last. The harbor we had sailed into was full of Swedish warships on whose decks sailors waved and shouted "Valkommen" [Welcome].

It took money, and lots of it, to save the Danish Jews. A number of fishermen asked high prices, some did it for nothing, and the rest took a modest fee. All told, the crossings cost about $600,000. The minority of affluent Jews could pay their own way, and many helped pay for others too. The majority had to sell possessions to raise the money. Those who had nothing to sell were given funds raised by the underground movement or other Danish rescue groups. One of the largest rescue funds was set up by the business associations. No one was left behind for lack of money.

Life for the Germans stationed in Denmark during the war was quite comfortable. Rather than see it disturbed, many accepted bribes to cooperate in rescues, or at least to look the other way. The German commander of the port of Copenhagen even saw to it that his coastal patrol vessels were put up for repairs just at the time the rescue operations took place. It was publicly known that the Germans did little to interfere with the flight of the Jews.

Of course some Jews and their helpers did get caught. One family was at sea in their own boat when the engine broke down and a Danish captain took them aboard his vessel. He turned them in to the Germans, who sent them all to the Theresienstadt ghetto in Czechoslovakia. Here and there others were captured. But only once was a large group taken. Acting on the tip of an informer, the Gestapo seized 110 Jews awaiting boats in a fishing harbor. About 200 others hid successfully until the Gestapo left and then escaped to Sweden. All together, some 275 were captured while trying to flee Denmark, about thirty others were drowned when boats capsized in stormy weather, and perhaps another thirty killed themselves in despair.

Although the Danish police were under the orders of the German occupation, they gave their allegiance to the moral law. They pretended to pursue the refugees at sea while actually they escorted their boats to safety. Then they turned in false reports to mislead the Germans.

In a tiny span of time the Danes transferred almost 8,000 Jews across the sea to Sweden and safety. Less than

600 had been captured by the Nazis and sent to the Theresienstadt ghetto. Because of constant pressure by the Danish government, no Danish Jews were sent from the ghetto to the gas chambers.

A historian of this extraordinary moment in history, Leni Yahil, reveals the interplay of the German and Danish characters that helped make possible the success of the rescue:

The Danes showed great aptitude in exploiting the psychological weaknesses of the Germans: their blind faith in every piece of paper with an official stamp on it; their haughtiness, of which the Danes made use by intrigues in which they made themselves out as fools; their love of money and their enthusiasm for Danish delicatessen, beer, etc.; the remnants of conscience left in them and the need even of Gestapo agents to appear as decent people in Danish eyes. As a result of this psychological perception the "stupid Danes" carried out the most daring and dangerous operations, and often a long time went by before the Germans realized that they had been hoodwinked. Then of course their anger knew no bounds and they did not rest until they had carried out their revenge. Audacity springing from coolness and realistic imagination guided by alert observation—these were the hallmarks of the Danish underground fighters; and it first became clear in October 1943 that these qualities were the preserve of many Danes among all sections of the population. The professor and the fisherman, the doctor and the taxi driver, the priest and the policeman—all understood each other without as much as saying a word.

8 A Legend Among Jews

What happened in Denmark was an astonishing—and singular—example of a nation identifying itself with Hitler's Jewish victims and rescuing almost all of them.

In Hungary the world witnessed an astounding example of another kind: the ability of one individual to bring about the rescue of tens of thousands of Jews.

His name was Raoul Wallenberg. His father, a young Swedish naval officer, died of cancer just before Raoul was born. Raoul's paternal grandfather, Gustav Wallenberg, a diplomat, took over the boy's upbringing when Raoul's mother remarried. After high school and brief compulsory military service, Raoul was sent to France for a year to add French to his English, German, and Russian. Then he studied architecture in the United States. At the University of Michigan he was rated one of the best and brightest students.

Returning to Sweden, he began to study commerce and banking at his grandfather's insistence. For six months he worked for a Swedish firm in South Africa, and then for a Dutch bank in Palestine. There, living in a kosher boarding house, he met several young Jews who had fled

Hitler's Germany. What he learned from them of Nazi persecution moved him deeply—not only because he was a warm, sympathetic man, but also because he knew his great-great-grandfather on his mother's side had been a Jew, one of the first to settle in Sweden, and had converted to the Lutheran faith and risen to become financial advisor to the king. His son was a founder of the Swedish steel industry. Raoul was proud of his Jewish heritage. He once told a friend that as a Wallenberg and a partial Jew he would "never be defeated."

Raoul grew into a self-confident young man, handsome, likeable, brave. Soon after he came back to Sweden from Palestine, his grandfather died. The pressure on Raoul relaxed. But what should he do now? He liked architecture, yet with an American diploma he could not practice in Sweden. Besides, with the great depression of the 1930s affecting Sweden too, little building was going on. He did not care to enter the family's banking business. The war had started, but Sweden was neutral. After floundering awhile, Raoul entered an export-import firm, dealing in specialty foods. He was made junior partner to the owner, Koloman Lauer, a Hungarian Jew. As a Gentile, Raoul was valuable, for unlike Lauer, he could travel freely to do business in Germany as well as in Nazi-occupied countries. There he got to know how Nazis thought and operated, in both business and government. At home he lived a comfortable bachelor's life, enjoying his many friends.

But his life in the business world did not satisfy him. What did it matter, this buying and selling of delicatessen products inside a Europe dominated by the Nazis? As a citizen of a neutral country he could do little about it, except to help in relief work for refugees who had escaped to Sweden. It depressed him to sit by while these terrible things were being done by the Germans.

Then in June 1944 came the chance to break out of his frustration. He was asked to go to Hungary to help get as many Jews as possible out of Hitler's hands and into Sweden. He would go with a diplomatic passport and plenty of money to carry out the work.

What was going on in Hungary at this time? Hungary, a small country in eastern-central Europe, had been part of the huge Austro-Hungarian empire that had been defeated in World War I. Pieces of the empire were torn away by treaties after the war, and large numbers of Hungarian minorities ended up in neighboring countries. A small Hungarian nation remained, operating as a monarchy, with Admiral Nicolas Horthy as regent.

Before World War I Hungary was less infected with anti-Semitism than most eastern and central European countries. It was the loss of territories as a result of defeat in that war that gave Hungarian anti-Semites an opening in the press and politics for their hate propaganda. In 1938, after swallowing up Austria, Hungary's neighbor, Hitler applied enormous pressure, and the Horthy government appeased him with some anti-Jewish decrees.

When World War II began, Hungary joined Germany as an ally. Hitler let her retain her "independence," instead of installing his own puppet government, and let her troops take over some of her lost territories. Still, Horthy avoided joining in the scheme for the "final solution." Hungarian troops did carry out some pogroms against Jews, but thousands of desperate Jews from Nazi-occupied Poland, Czechoslovakia, and other areas continued to cross into "independent" Hungary in the hope of shelter.

Some 800,000 Jews were inside Hungary by 1943. The Nazis demanded that the Hungarians surrender the Jews for deportation. But Admiral Horthy, knowing the Jews would end up in the gas chambers, stalled. In March 1944 Hitler decided to force the issue and sent in troops to occupy the country. Horthy's cabinet resigned—although he remained—and a puppet regime took over, eager to please Hitler. It issued sweeping anti-Jewish decrees, set up ghettos, and began deportations. The death trains from all over the land headed for Auschwitz. In a few months the Germans deported 435,000 Jews from the provinces. Meanwhile, Adolf Eichmann prepared a plan to round up the Jews in Budapest, the capital.

The Jewish Council of Hungary appealed to the world to do something to halt the deportations. It especially sought help from the neutral countries and organizations—Sweden, Switzerland, Portugal, the Vatican, the International Red Cross. It was then that Raoul Wallenberg's partner, Lauer, proposed to a committee of prominent Swedish Jews that Wallenberg was the Gentile they sought for a rescue mission to Budapest. Wallenberg was eager to leave the safety of neutral Sweden to undertake this perilous challenge to Hitler's power. The Swedish goverment agreed and made him a special envoy with diplomatic protection. He knew all about the workings of diplomats and bureaucrats, how their caution, their stodginess, their red tape could strangle the swift action this emergency demanded. He insisted upon the promise of a free hand to use any methods he saw fit—by which he meant bribery, the right to deal with anyone he wished

106

to no matter who or what they were, and the authority to give asylum to persons holding Swedish protective passes in buildings belonging to the Swedish legation. Both the prime minister and the king accepted his conditions. The Swedes, the surviving Hungarian Jews, the War Refugee Board of the United States, all provided funds for Wallenberg's mission.

Even before Raoul left Sweden, the neutral missions in Budapest had begun to take random steps to protect some Jews. The Swedes, for instance, had already given 650 protective passes to Jews with family or business ties to Sweden. Raoul saw how he could take advantage of the fact that the Germans were losing the war and on the retreat everywhere. Both the German and the Hungarian officials in Budapest were worried about postwar punishment. They would be open to persuasion, threats, bribery, and blackmail.

But in Budapest, at the luxurious Hotel Majestic, sat Adolf Eichmann, now thirty-eight years old and the SS officer in charge of Hitler's Jewish deportations. He had done duty in all the other occupied countries of Europe, using his special talent for the relentless organization of mass murder. He felt dedicated to destroying every Jew he could lay his hands on before the war ended. "Any compromise, even the slightest, will have to be paid for bitterly at a later date," he said. He had already gone a long way toward destroying the 800,000 Jews of Hungary.

Only 230,000 Jews were left, trapped in Budapest. Eichmann, proud of his success in deporting the meticulously counted 437,402 Jewish men, women, and children from the provinces, planned a swift roundup of the capital's Jews. But Horthy, still the regent, was impressed by the

107

protests from abroad and fearful of the advancing Russian army. He ordered a stop to the deportations. He sent the 1,600 Hungarian troops Eichmann needed for a roundup back to the provinces. And now Eichmann would also come up against the will and courage of another man just as powerfully dedicated as he, but dedicated to the saving—not the destruction—of human life.

Raoul Wallenberg left Sweden for Budapest via Berlin, wearing a long leather coat and a soft hat, and carrying a rucksack with some clothes. In his pocket he had a small revolver—"not for use," he said, "but to give myself courage." His first step in Budapest was to establish "Section C" at the Swedish embassy; its sole purpose was to rescue Jews. He designed a new and far more impressive Swedish passport to replace the casual certificates issued thus far. He dressed the passport up with the Royal Swedish crown, seals, stamps, and his signature. It had no validity in international law, but it made German and Hungarian bureaucrats believe its holders were not abandoned outcasts, but rather the protected wards of a major neutral power. The Jews who were given the passports felt hope again; they were no longer to be treated as things, but as respected human beings.

Raoul induced the German and Hungarian officials to accept first a few, then hundreds, then thousands of these passports. Soon other neutrals followed in his path, issuing protective passports, and the underground began turning out counterfeit passports on a large scale. Raoul gathered 250 Jews, largely volunteers working day and night in shifts to handle the people pouring in for the lifesaving documents.

To help Jews desperately in need, Raoul set up children's shelters, clinics, nurseries, and soup kitchens, and bought the food, clothing, and medicine to stock them. He rented or bought buildings and housed Jews under Swedish protection. He financed these projects with the ample funds supplied by the American Joint Distribution Committee and the War Refugee Board, and by the International Red Cross. Raoul's staff rose to 400, as he coordinated all relief and rescue efforts sponsored by a joint committee of neutrals. He could never snatch more than a few hours sleep at night. His devotion, his energy, and his organizing skill inspired everyone around him. No low-key diplomat, he was "working like hell," wrote one observer.

Although Horthy had ordered all deportations to stop, Eichmann still managed to deport 1,500 prominent Jews held in a detention camp to Auschwitz. He brought 10,000 SS troops to Budapest to prepare for a lightning roundup of the rest of the Jews late in August. Getting word of this, the tireless Wallenberg had all the neutral missions in Budapest issue a strong protest. And again Horthy forbade deportations and threatened to use Hungarian troops and police to stop it by force. On orders from Heinrich Himmler, Eichmann backed away.

As Allied planes made bombing raids over Budapest, Horthy decided he would secretly seek a separate peace. He insisted that the Germans return control of Jewish affairs to his government and that Eichmann and his SS forces be withdrawn. This extraordinary show of independence from a satellite country, combined with the recent bomb plot that had almost killed Hitler and the collapse of his Romanian ally, led the shaky Nazis to agree. Eichmann left for Berlin. Wallenberg believed the worst was about over and began to plan his return home.

But it was not over. Warned of Horthy's secret negotiations for a separate peace, the Nazis suddenly sent troops back into Hungary, forced Horthy to leave for Berlin, and placed Ferenc Szálasi, the leader of the Hungarian Nazi party, the Arrow Cross, in power.

In Berlin, Eichmann was still cooking up plans to carry out the Budapest deportation. Rather than use the trains the retreating German troops badly needed, he would deport the Hungarian Jews on foot. He headed back to Budapest.

The first night the Arrow Cross government was in power, many Jews were arrested and disappeared. Budapest Jews, living in houses marked by a yellow star, were ordered to stay in their homes. Jews who ventured out were murdered in the streets. Fascist gangs, often teenagers, invaded homes, looting, flogging, and killing Jews. Wallenberg organized strong young Hungarian Jews into commando squads to protect blockaded Jews and bring them food and medicine.

Then the new government announced it would no longer recognize the protection offered Jews by the neutral missions and the churches. No letters of safe conduct or foreign passports for Hungarian Jews from whatever source would permit Jews to escape the "solution of the Jewish problem."

Thousands of Jews who had hoped to survive with these documents were threatened by the order. Wallenberg moved at once to counteract it. He reached Baroness Elizabeth Kemény, the wife of the Minister of Foreign Affairs; he knew her to be of Jewish birth, a fact not generally known in Budapest. By marrying the Hungarian baron, whose Fascist sympathies she did not know of at the time, she had become an "honorary Aryan." He urged her to induce her husband to have the government's order rescinded. He pointed out that the Soviet army was almost at the gates of Budapest. When the city fell, he warned, the government leaders would all be hanged as war criminals—except, of course, for those who acted humanely. Then he told her he was aware of her Jewish origins and appealed to her sympathy for the suffering of the Jews. His use of both threats and promises succeeded. She got her husband to convince Szálasi to act. The government announced over the radio that it would recognize the documents issued by the neutrals to the Jews.

The number of Jews protected by documents was about 16,000. What of all the others, the nearly 200,000 without papers? Eichmann and the Fascist government still meant to murder them. Late in October 1944 Eichmann rounded up some 35,000 Jewish men between the ages of sixteen and sixty—except those with Wallenberg passports—and marched them off to the outskirts of Budapest to dig trenches and build earthwork defenses to hold up the Russian army. No matter what their physical condition, they were forced to do backbreaking labor. Many died of it.

The women and children were next on Eichmann's list. Wallenberg and the neutrals did their best to stop him, but he began deportations, on foot, on November 8. It was the first of the death marches along a 120-mile route west from the capital to the Austrian border. (They went west because the rail system east to Auschwitz had collapsed and the killing camp was soon to be closed.) In freezing rain, the women and children walked twenty to twenty-five miles a day, with the Hungarians whipping those who faltered. If they dropped, they died in the ditches. Often there was no shelter at night, no food, no water, no cot. They slept on the earth, and the weak froze to death. Many committed suicide. Even the convoys of German troops they met going the other way were appalled by the cruelty of the Hungarians. About 27,000 Jews were driven on foot to the border, then herded onto trains bound for a death camp. Among them were men from the labor battalions, who were sent to the borders by different routes.

It was during the forced marches of those terrible weeks that Wallenberg saved even more Jews. With some coworkers beside him, he rode tirelessly up and down that road, distributing food, medicine, and warm clothing to the hounded Jews. He carried his "book of life," a book with the names of Jews to whom passports had been issued, and blank passports as well, which he filled in and issued on the spot. On one such trip he saved about a hundred Jews, often using sheer bluff. Again and again he and his helpers made that journey; they rescued about 2,000 Jews, bringing them back to Budapest. He also rescued about 15,000 labor service men who also held Swedish and other protective papers.

One of the survivors of those marches, Zvi Eres, recalls how he (then fourteen years old), his mother, an aunt, and a cousin were saved by Raoul:

As we approached Hegyeshalom at the end of the march, we saw two men standing by the side of the road. One of them, wearing a long leather coat and a fur hat, told us he was from the Swedish legation and asked if we had Swedish passports. If we hadn't, he said, perhaps they had been taken away from us or torn up by the Arrow Cross men. We were on our last legs, but alert enough to take the hint and we said, yes, that was exactly what had happened, though in fact none of us had ever had a Swedish Schutzpass. He put our names down on a list and we walked on. At the station later we again saw Wallenberg and some of his assistants, among them— as I learned only later—some members of the Zionist youth movement, posing as Red Cross officials, and representatives of the papal nuncio. A group of Hungarian officers and Germans in SS uniforms were there, too. Wallenberg was brandishing his list, obviously demanding that everybody on it should be allowed to go. Voices were raised and they were shouting at each other in German. It was too far away for me to hear exactly what was being said, but clearly there was a tremendous argument going on. In the end, to our amazement, Wallenberg won his point and between 280 and 300 of us were allowed to go back to Budapest.

Raoul's courage was tried against the greatest odds. Once an armed patrol of Arrow Cross men invaded a group of Swedish protected houses and began to drag the Jews out. Raoul raced to the district and shouted, "This is Swedish protected territory! If you want to take them you will have to shoot me first!" The patrol let the Jews go. Another time, word came that eleven Jews with Swedish passports had been forced onto a train headed for Austria. He chased the train in his diplomatic car, caught up with it just as it reached the border, and got the eleven people released.

By early December the Russians had entered the suburbs of Budapest. As Allied bombers pounded the city, food and fuel were almost impossible to find, and disease spread everywhere. The Jews were jammed into two areas: the holders of protective passports in the protected houses, and others in the enclosed ghetto. With law and order gone, bands of thugs looted Jewish homes, raped the women, tortured and murdered the men.

Raoul was everywhere in this chaos. He was "a legend among the Jews," wrote one survivor. "In the complete and total hell in which we lived, there was a savior-angel somewhere, moving around." His courage and the power of his extraordinary personality worked miracles. Yet he stood alone, relying only on his personal authority. There was nothing to back him up.

He built a fine intelligence network out of friends, sustained by bribery and blackmail, a network that gave him instant notice of deportations, street assaults, and raids on protected houses. Again and again he turned up only with his driver, to face down German officers and Arrow Cross gangs and save the lives of Jews. In the midst of these last desperate weeks in Budapest he wrote a friend in Stockholm that he was "in good spirits and eager for the fray." To his mother he wrote, "I hope that the longed-for peace is not too distant."

With the Russian troops battering their way into the heart of the city, hundreds of SS and Arrow Cross men converged on the two districts holding the Jews. They were determined to wipe them out in the little time left to them. Raoul warned the German commander that unless he used his troops to stop the slaughter, he would be hanged for the crime. His threat worked. The final massacre was averted as the Russians broke through and captured the city in February 1945.

About 144,000 Jews survived in Budapest. They were the only Jewish community of considerable size left in Europe. Half the Jews of prewar Hungary were annihilated. As the survivors looked for Wallenberg to show him their gratitude, he was nowhere to be found. Later it was learned that he had gone to meet the Russian commander, Marshal Malinovsky, to ask for relief assistance for the Jews. But instead of welcoming him as a hero, the Russians had taken him into custody. He disappeared. He was never heard from again. Despite continued pressure from those trying to determine his fate, the Russians reported nothing until 1957, when they said he had died in a Russian prison in 1947. But reports persisted that he was alive somewhere inside Soviet prison walls.

Why the Russians seized him no one knows. It may be that they believed this saver of souls was a spy.

9 Fear Nothing

Italy was ruled by the Fascist dictator Benito Mussolini for ten years before Hitler seized power in Germany. Both men were Fascists in their politics, but yet the people they ruled over behaved in vastly different ways. Especially with regard to the Jews.

Most Italian Jews were assimilated and well-educated middle-class people. Their families had lived in Italy for generations. Indeed, before the birth of Christ some 8,000 Jews were settled on the banks of the Tiber in Rome. In the early Christian era and in the Middle Ages the Jews of Italy suffered persecution and restriction. The period of the Italian Renaissance—the early 1500s to the mid 1600s—was less oppressive, but later in the seventeenth century Jews were confined to ghettos in most Italian cities as well as throughout Europe.

The degrading life in the ghetto lasted over 200 years. Not until the unification of Italy in the mid-nineteenth century did complete emancipation come. Rapidly Jews earned prominence and influence in politics and the military, in the arts and sciences, and in commerce and industry. They became fully accepted in national life. Jews looked, dressed, talked, and acted like other Italians of their class. When discrimination disappeared, some Jews abandoned their religious heritage. But many, though feeling fully Italian, cherished their Jewish traditions and Jewish values.

When Mussolini rose to power in 1922, he did not turn the country back to anti-Semitism. Only a small group in his Fascist party were anti-Semitic. Mussolini himself called anti-Semitism "an alien weed that cannot strike roots in Italy where Jews are citizens with full equality." Nevertheless, most Jews opposed Mussolini and what Fascism stood for. Some of them risked their livelihood and their safety to fight the dictatorship.

After observing Hitler in power, Mussolini saw how effective anti-Semitism could be as a political tool. Although Mussolini had previously denounced racism, he now had his controlled press mount attacks on the Jews, and in 1938 he began to issue anti-Semitic decrees. The Italian people showed their contempt for such measures. Enforcement of the laws was slow and lax. Still, many Jews suffered—although, compared with Germany, their plight was bearable. They did not wear the yellow badges, and most could still work. They were not ostracized, and they were not penned up in ghettos.

But some 7,000 Jews did not wait around for the worst to happen; they fled the country by the fall of 1941. A few months later, foreign Jews living in Italy were interned in a few camps, and some Italian Jews were called up for labor. By this time the Nazis were issuing instructions throughout occupied Europe for mass deportations. But Hitler shied away from telling Mussolini what to do.

With the Allied landing in Sicily in July 1943, Mussolini fell from power. A new government led by Marshall Badoglio surrendered to the Allies in a few weeks. The Germans disarmed the Italian troops and occupied the country. The Allies moved up the boot, in hard fighting, but the Germans held Naples, Rome, and about two thirds of Italy. They set up a puppet regime to do Hitler's bidding. Now the Jews of Italy were in the gravest danger.

Deportation orders were issued. The first targets were the Jews of Rome. Many had gone into hiding when the Germans entered the city. The Italians, appalled by the deportation action, opened their homes to Jewish friends and strangers. High administration officials helped. The police commander, Mario de Marco, resisted orders to hand over Jewish registration lists and arranged false identity cards for the Jews. He saved hundreds of lives. Arrested and tortured by the Gestapo, he did not yield his secrets. Another police chief, Doctor Giovanni Polatucci, of Fiume, who helped many Jews, was deported to Dachau and killed. The Cardinal of Genoa set up a network to rescue Jews, and other church officials protested Hitler's policy. But the pope was silent, much to the Nazis' relief. On October 15 the grand roundup of Rome's Jews began, and lasted for twenty-four hours. The Germans succeeded in capturing 1,000 Jews—the other 7,000 had been warned in time and were hidden, often in monasteries, convents, or other church buildings. Many priests were arrested, and some died for helping to save the innocents.

News of the roundup spread immediately through Rome, before the Jews were put on trains for Auschwitz. But only by word of mouth. None of the newspapers reported it. Nor did a single government official try to stop the German action against Italian citizens. Pope Pius XII seems

119

to have been informed in advance of the order to arrest and deport the Roman Jews. But "before the roundup," says the historian Susan Zuccotti, "he never threatened, suggested, or even hinted that he would publicly condemn any SS action to deport the Jews of his own city." Long before October he had learned that death awaited deported Jews. Churchmen from all over Europe had confirmed the reports of death camps. Nor did the pope make public protest even after the roundup occurred. Fortunately many Catholics in Rome—both clergy and lay—did not wait for his word; they were already doing their best to protect Jews.

If the pope had spoken out, it would have helped save Jews from raids in other Italian cities in the months that followed. More Jews might have grasped the terrible reality of their fate and fled their homes to find safety. And with guidance from the pope, more Catholics might have acted to shelter Jews. The power of a papal condemnation of the Holocaust might have had even greater effect upon other Nazi-occupied countries.

Why didn't the pope act? Perhaps because he feared a strong attack upon Hitler's "final solution" might cause the Germans to occupy the Vatican and seize church properties throughout Italy. It might provoke reprisals on Catholics in all German-occupied countries. And finally, some suggest the pope felt his first responsibility was to protect and preserve the institution of the church. A threat to excommunicate Catholics who killed Jews might bring many German Catholics to quit the church.

Although he failed to publicly condemn the Holocaust, priests, nuns, and bishops risked their lives to hide thousands of Jews, and certainly the pope knew of it. Although he did little to encourage their defense of the Jews, he did not stop it.

What happened about one hundred miles north of Rome in the hill town of Assisi—known worldwide as the home of Saint Francis—exemplifies the courage of such Italian priests. Father Rufino Niccacci, a thirty-two-year-old peasant turned priest, was the head of the seminary in Assisi. A happy man who loved good food and wine, he wanted only to serve God, Saint Francis, and the people Saint Francis had devoted his life to. A few hours after Rome fell to the Germans in September 1943, his life changed radically. Bishop Nicolini asked him to take care of some refugees hiding in the town, for many Italian Catholics had taken to the roads when their towns were bombed and their homes destroyed. But *these* men and women, disguised as Christian pilgrims, were not Catholics. They were Jews who had fled north when the Germans moved into Rome. They were the very first Jews Father Rufino had ever laid eyes on, for no Jew before this time had ever settled in Assisi.

That was the beginning of the priest's new mission as "Father Guardian of the Jews." Over the next nine months he would protect 300 Jews who came to Assisi. He hid them in twenty-six monasteries and convents in and around the town. Those who did not look Jewish or speak with an obvious foreign accent were taken into the private homes of his parishioners, many of whom already had Catholic refugees lodged with them. But they welcomed the new ones, and without any pay. Father Rufino furnished them with false identity cards and found jobs that blended them into the community. A local printer, Luigi Brizi, and his son, Trento, turned their skills to the secret printing of false documents that were so superbly made they were soon being sent by courier to Jews all over Italy. Father Rufino set up two clandestine schools in Assisi. In one, trusted clerics with teaching experience conducted academic classes so that Jewish children would not lose a year because of the German occupation. In the other, the Jews were taught how to behave as Christians and given a special seminar in catechism and liturgy so that they could walk about the streets and attend church without arousing suspicion.

So successful was the masquerade that one of the Jewish refugees was able to go into business with the town pharmacist, a Fascist, and supply him with the medicines that he somehow got hold of in a time of terrible shortages. He also managed to publicly court his Jewish sweetheart at the best hotel, and exchange greetings daily with the local dignitaries, right under the eyes of German officers. Another Jewish woman became Assisi's leading religious artist, painting such beautiful scenes from the saints' lives that German Catholic soldiers eagerly paid high prices for them.

That winter Clara Weiss, a Jewish woman suffering from diabetes, died as she lay hidden in a cloister. She could not be buried as a Jew without exposing the conspiracy to conceal Jews. So Father Rufino arranged for a burial certificate attesting to the fact that Signora Carla Bianchi, the Catholic refugee from Foggia, had died of diabetes, and she was placed in a coffin in the cloister. Refugees and nuns and priests gathered in the cloister while ten Jewish men donned their skullcaps and said Kaddish, the prayer for the dead and for the living that remain behind. The coffin was closed and placed on a two-horse carriage draped in black. The procession moved through the winding, rainy streets to the cemetery on the edge of town.

There, at the edge of the grave, a priest read from the New Testament and delivered a eulogy praising the life of Signora Bianchi, who had never forgotten the poor and needy in her seventy years in Foggia and never missed a Sunday mass. And then Clara Weiss was laid to rest, the only Jew in that hallowed ground.

One night the long-suspicious SS raided the Jews' hideaways. But warned by informers in Gestapo headquarters, the refugees, escorted by priests and partisans, fled in time into the forests and mountains. Many found new hiding places with peasants living in remote places. Those who did not look Jewish hid in other towns. On June 17, 1944, the Allied troops reached Assisi and liberated the town. Not a single Jewish refugee was captured in Assisi. No one who shared in the rescue operation ever betrayed it.

Long after, Father Rufino said that in those months he became "a cheat and a liar—for a good cause, mind you, but nevertheless a sinner, although I am sure that I have long since made my peace with God and that He has forgiven my trespasses." He died in 1977, at the age of sixty-six.

Throughout northern Italy at this time there lived about 35,000 Jews. Most of them hid in small villages that were hard for the SS to penetrate. The Germans began a systematic hunt for them, and in the spring of 1944 deported the 7,000 they captured to death camps. Popular resistance and aid to the Jews helped weaken this attempt at extermination, even though almost one-fifth of the Italian Jews in the north were killed.

During the war Italian troops occupied parts of south-ern France, Croatia, and Yugoslavia. While on duty in these places officers in the Italian army, or in the Italian Foreign Service, showed great generosity toward the Jews, never telling Mussolini what they were doing, and some-times acting in direct opposition to his orders.

Italians, not Germans, occupied the city of Nice on the French Riviera, where about 50,000 Jews had clustered. They could only hope that the Italians would be more humane than the Germans, and not deliver them up for deportation. But at the end of 1942 the French Vichy officials ordered all foreign Jews to be shipped to the northern zone of France occupied by the Nazis. Everyone knew that from there the Jews would be deported east to the death camps.

But Angelo Donati, an Italian Jew with friends high in the Italian government and the Vatican, intervened. He got the Italian consul in Nice to urge the Foreign Ministry in Rome to resist the persecution of the Jews in the Ital-ian-occupied territory. The Jews rejoiced at this astound-ing turn of events: an ally of Hitler protecting them from Hitler! The Jews of Nice saw the chance to aid Jews in other parts of France controlled by the Nazis. They began smuggling Jews into this sanctuary—however temporary it might be—in southern France. They raised large funds, prepared forged documents, made contacts with the un-derground, sought out the smugglers to bring Jews over from the German-occupied zone, and found food, cloth-ing, and places for them to live.

This enraged the Germans and the French anti-Semites. But the Italians insisted on asserting their authority in the region they occupied. When the French anti-Semites began physically attacking Jews, the Italian military stationed guards around the synagogue in Nice. When the French prefect refused to legalize the stay of newly arrived Jews and wouldn't issue them identity or ration cards, the Italian army gave the Jewish committee in Nice the right to issue its own documents and threatened to arrest any French policemen who refused to honor them.

The Italians took another bold step to defy the Nazis and their French collaborators. The Vichy government decreed that all documents issued to the Jews bear the stamp *juif* (Jew). The Italian military refused to allow the order to be applied to Italian Jews or to Polish, Czech, Austrian, or even German Jews. All of them, they said, are stateless refugees under our protection.

When it was rumored that Italy would surrender and quit the alliance with Hitler to join the Allies, the Jews in southern France hoped to flee into Italy. There they would be safely out of Hitler's reach, they thought. The Badoglio government agreed to admit 30,000 Jews, pending permission from the Allies it was secretly dealing with. Thousands of Jews flocked into Nice to await transport to Italy. But for whatever reasons, that permission was held up. When the Allies prematurely announced the sensational news of the Italian armistice, the Germans rushed troops into southern France. A few hundred Jews fled with the Italian forces, only to be seized later by the Germans and killed.

In Nice the Germans and the French anti-Semites hunted down Jews, raiding homes and hotels day and night. They stopped men they suspected of being Jewish on the street and forced them to strip. If they were circumcised (circumcision at that time was not routine, and was done only as part of a Jewish rite), they were beaten up and taken to an assembly point. Many of those in hiding were exposed by informers in return for German rewards. The roundup in southern France was as brutal as in the ghettos of Poland, and the thousands captured died in Auschwitz.

Italian soldiers stationed in Croatia displayed the same humane concern for refugee Jews as did their counterparts in southern France. The majority of Croatians, however, were cruel to the Jews. In 1941 young Ivo Herzer was caught with his family and about a dozen other Jews in a small Croatian town. They hoped somehow to travel north and to cross the border into Italy. Herzer recalls what happened:

The situation seemed to be hopeless. But, by chance, a few Italian soldiers who were garrisoned there passed the house where we were staying, and my father, just on intuition, approached them and told them two words. He did not know that much Italian but he said simply, "Ebrei paura" [Jews fear]. The soldiers immediately reacted and answered, "Niente paura," which means "Fear nothing." Soon, their sergeant arrived. He spoke a little French and told us that he would try to get us on an Italian Army train bound for Italy and thereby, of course, save our lives.

We didn't believe him, but at midnight that night he came with a few soldiers, none of whom we had seen before, who did not demand money or any promises, but escorted us to the railroad station and put us on an Italian Army train. They actually boarded the train with us.

The train was full of Italian soldiers, surprised to see this bunch of 12 or 15 bedraggled civilians running away.

But somehow, he was able to explain to them, probably using the words "refugees," "poor people," or even "Jews." I don't know how he did it. I didn't speak Italian at the time, but he managed to get us across the border into the Italian city of Fiume.

But the sergeant didn't stop there. He went to the authorities, asked that we be given food and drink, which was promptly given, and then he took leave. I don't know his name, but I do know that hundreds of Croatian Jews were helped to escape from Croatia, where only death awaited them, into the Italian zone by men like this sergeant.

Later, Herzer's family was taken to a camp on the coast. They feared that the Italians, pressured by the Nazis, were about to turn them over. But the Italians stalled off the Germans and let the Jews organize the camp into a real community. They held religious services, ran their own schools, and were provided with rations. Most of the Jews in that camp survived the war, thanks to Italian protection.

It is estimated that 85 percent of the Italian Jews were saved. About 32,000 Italian Jews and several thousand foreign Jews were hidden successfully by the Italian people. That survival rate was among the highest in occupied Europe. To what can it be attributed? Both objective circumstances and personal factors help explain it.

For one thing, deportation in Italy began much later than in the other countries, and the period of danger was shorter: only nine months in Rome and twenty months in central and northern Italy. Then, too, Italian Jews were but a tiny part of the population—one tenth of 1 percent—so the need for help was not overwhelming, as it was in countries with much bigger Jewish populations. Most of Italy's Jews were well off and had not been impoverished by long imprisonment in ghettos. Money eased the way to survival. So did the fact that Italian Jews looked like any other Italians; they could pass easily. A great many Jews, like other Italians, were resourceful, used to making up their own minds, not dependent upon authority, willing to bend the rules if need be. When they understood the nature of the crisis, they acted quickly to save themselves.

But they could not have succeeded without the aid of the men and women of the church, the professions, and the government, and of workers, farmers, and housewives. To those outstretched hands, to their own courage and daring, and to the unpredictable gift of good luck, the survivors owed their lives.

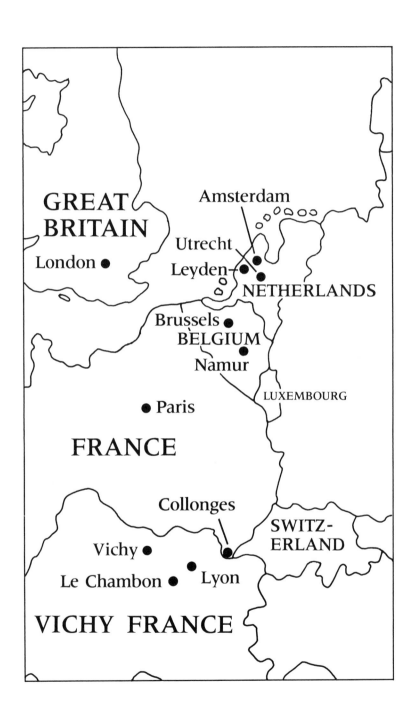

10   It Was the Right Thing to Do

The Low Countries—Holland and Belgium—fell to the Nazi war machine in May 1940. The lives of the Jews in this northwestern corner of Europe were quite unlike the lives of those in Eastern Europe. The Dutch Jews were only 1.6 percent of the population. They spoke the same language as all the Dutch. They shared in a common culture. They looked the same and dressed the same as their neighbors. Long ago they had stopped wearing the beards and the caftans of eastern Jews. The ghettos had been dissolved a century ago, and now the Jews lived and moved freely among non-Jews. Only in Amsterdam was there a relatively high Jewish population of 10 percent. The Jews considered themselves citizens with the same rights and obligations as all others, and they were accepted as such by most of the Dutch. Anti-Semitism was not unknown, but there was only a small Dutch Nazi movement.

The Germans took tight hold in Holland, putting their own Nazis in charge. They fired Jews from public office and excluded them from the professions. Jewish business firms either collapsed or were taken over. Both rich and middle-class Jews were forced into poverty.

Next, Jewish teachers were dismissed and Jewish students segregated. When Professor R. P. Cleevringa of Leyden University protested the dismissal of a Jewish colleague, he was sent to a concentration camp. The students at Leyden and other universities went on strike against the firing of Jewish faculty. Some student groups dissolved rather than ban their Jewish members.

Early in 1941 the Germans provoked the first anti-Jewish riot in Amsterdam. Dutch Nazis led by German SS men marched on the old Jewish quarter, smashing windows, dragging Jews off trolley cars, setting fire to synagogues, and attacking pedestrians. After the initial shock, the Jews fought back with iron bars, clubs, and fists. Christian neighbors joined in their defense and forced the Nazis to retreat. That night the Nazis came back in greater numbers. But Christian factory workers and longshoremen joined the Jewish fighters, while Christian women sheltered Jewish children and Christian doctors treated the injured. Again the Dutch Nazis were beaten back. Angered by the unexpected resistance, the Germans used automatic weapons and tanks to put it down ruthlessly.

A few days later the SS seized 425 young Jews on the streets and shipped them to Mauthausen camp, where they were killed. The Dutch were enraged. In Amsterdam several thousand workers went on strike to protest the deportation of Jews as well as the sending of any Dutch citizens into forced labor. The rebellion spread; shipyards, armaments factories, transport systems, and utilities were struck in two other cities as well.

This was the only time in occupied Europe that workers would strike to protest the persecution of Jews. The Germans were astonished, but they soon crushed the strikes. They declared martial law, arrested workers wholesale, and sent many off to concentration camps.

The first step toward deportation, the registration of all Jews, had already been decreed. Now the letter "J" was added to identity cards, and ghetto sections were set up. Then Jews were ordered to wear yellow stars. (In sympathy, many Dutch Gentiles put yellow flowers in their lapels.) Jews could not shop in Gentile stores, or go to movies, concerts, museums, beaches, or use public transportation or taxis.

The churches were not silent in the face of Jewish persecution. They urged their parishioners to resist it, no matter what the cost. As one pastoral letter put it:

We know what conflicts of conscience result for those concerned. In order, therefore, to eliminate all doubts and uncertainties that you may have in this respect, we hereby declare most explicitly that no compromise in this domain of conscience is allowed; and should refusal of collaboration cause sacrifice to you, then remain steadfast in the certainty that you are fulfilling your duty toward God and man.

It was this spirit that moved Christians to help.

Holland was a hard place for Jews to hide in. Flat, marshy, without woods or caves, and very small, there was almost no natural place for concealment. To escape abroad was even harder: Exit was cut off by Germany on one side, occupied Belgium on another, and the open sea to the west and north. Still, Dutch Christians by the thousands

133

bravely risked everything to save Jews. They hid them in cellars and attics and closets, in homes and offices and warehouses, in cloisters and orphanages. A grocer, Leendert Hordijk, sheltered five Jews in his home in a small town, and for three years shared his meager rations with them. He was lucky. Twenty thousand other Dutch Christians were sent to concentration camps for trying to block Nazi racism.

The young Jewish girl Anne Frank, as many millions the world over now know, described in her diary how Christians hid her family and friends for over two years. The members of the Frank family were among the many thousands of Jewish refugees from Germany and Austria who were welcomed by the Dutch before the war. For centuries Holland had offered the persecuted a refuge: French Huguenots in the sixteenth century, English Puritans in the seventeenth. Now, in 1934, it was Anne's family. Her father, Otto Frank, had set up a food products business in Amsterdam. When the Franks were summoned for deportation in July 1942, they went into hiding in a warehouse on the Prinsengracht Canal that had been prepared for this emergency.

It was a Dutch informer who caused their capture by the Germans in August 1944. Two of the Christians who hid them, Mr. Koophuis and Mr. Kraler, were also arrested. Mr. Koophuis was soon released because of his poor health, but Mr. Kraler spent eight months in a forced labor camp. Anne was sent to Auschwitz in the last deportation of Dutch Jews organized by Eichmann. From there she was moved to the Belsen camp in Germany. Starved, sick with typhus, she died in the country she was born in. She was not yet 16.

In so small a country as Holland it took great ingenuity

to help Jews disappear. A Utrecht student group devoted itself to finding hiding places for Jewish children, many of whom found safety in Christian homes until the end of the war. Another Dutch group specialized in counterfeiting identity papers for Jews. The Dutch resistance movement appealed to the entire nation for help:

Fellow countrymen: the deportation of all Jewish citizens . . . is the final link in the long chain of inhuman measures—It means the complete annihilation of the Jews. . . . The Netherlands has been deeply humiliated. . . . We must prove our honor is not lost and our conscience not silenced. . . . We ask our fellow Netherlanders to sabotage all preparations and executions of mass deportations. Remember the February strikes when an aroused people proved what it could do! We call upon burgomasters and high officials to risk their positions, if necessary, by refusing to cooperate with the Germans. We expect everyone in the position to do so to sabotage.

The Dutch Christians helped their Jewish compatriots, and they were often murdered for it. They went hungry, but they shared what little they had with Jews. Each day an average of 400 people died of starvation.

Husband and wife Joop and Will Westerweel stand out in Holland's story as André and Magda Trocmé do in France's. A Christian anarchist, pacifist, and teacher, in his youth Joop emigrated to the Dutch East Indies, where he worked for six years. His public protests against the exploitation of the Indonesians by the Dutch made the authorities glad to see him go.

Back in Holland, Joop opened a Montessori high school in Lundsrecht and became its principal. When the war began, he and his wife Will placed their four children in foster homes, quit their jobs, and joined the underground to resist the Nazi persecution of the Jews. They became the only Gentile members of a Zionist youth group formed in their town by two young teachers, Joachim Simon and his wife Adina. The group's work was to smuggle Jewish children into Switzerland. They cut trails through the mountains from France to the border. But the work went too slowly, so Simon went to France to develop contacts with the French underground and to work out a new route through the Pyrenees into neutral Spain. From Spain he hoped the children somehow could be sent to Palestine.

One day, returning to Holland from one of his perilous rescue missions, Simon was caught by the Gestapo. They tortured him to obtain the names of others in his group. Fearing he might give in, Simon slashed his wrists and died, silent to the end. Although now past the age of forty, Joop took over leadership of the rescue group. After a year of underground work, his wife Will was arrested, tortured, and sent to a concentration camp. Joop continued to lead Jewish children across the Low Countries, through the mountains of France, and into Spain. He returned after each mission to prepare at once for the next.

One child remembered what Joop said as he delivered them to safety: "Cross this difficult road successfully and build your homeland, a homeland for the whole Jewish people. But do not forget that you are bound to all humanity, something which you perhaps learned in Holland. Do not forget us, your non-Jewish comrades."

In the summer of 1944 Joop was captured as he tried to smuggle two Jewish girls out of a Nazi camp in Holland. He was flogged and sent to the camp in Vught. The underground managed to make contact with him through a Dutch camp doctor. For five months, while a plan was being worked out for his rescue, the Gestapo tortured this "Aryan" who dared to help Jews. In a note smuggled out of the camp by the physician, Joop told of his ordeal:

I was forced to remain on my feet from Thursday noon until Saturday noon without a break, my hands fettered and bound behind my back. I am in a tiny cell in a dark cellar. . . . My daily ration is four slices of bread and a bottle of tea. . . . They interrogate me, bind and beat me. . . . Each question is accompanied by blows and kicks. . . . They asked me if I cared to write a letter to my wife. I started eagerly to write but they stopped me and resumed the questioning. . . . I have a moment of respite. But on Monday it will start all over again. . . . I will not reveal any names to them; I am certain of this. I still feel strong. At night when there is a respite from the torture, my wounds have a chance to heal. Mornings when questions resume, I am rested and alert. I will remain silent. I am confident of this.

He never revealed a name. But before his rescue could be carried out, the doctor who was the link with the underground was exposed and executed. As the Germans took Joop into the woods to shoot him, he sang a freedom song he loved. His widow, freed by the Red Cross from a concentration camp after fifteen months there, survived the war.

Also in Holland there is the village of Niuvelande, as remarkable in its way as was the village of Le Chambon in France. Without help from any outsiders, the villagers decided that every home would conceal a Jew or a Jewish family. No one feared a neighbor would inform on them, for everyone was "guilty" of hiding a Jew.

A Jewish woman recorded in the documents only as "NRK," who migrated from Poland to Holland in 1938, lived out the German occupation in the town of Heerlen. She tells how, when the Germans began deportations, a Christian, Doctor De Jong, saved several hundred Jews by taking them into the municipal hospital. Tipped off whenever the Nazis were about to raid the wards looking for Jews, De Jong would sedate them till they lost consciousness, then tell the Nazis his patients were far too sick to be moved. NRK and her husband stayed three months under this protection.

One day a Dutch policeman named Jongen came to warn them that the Nazis planned to empty the hospital of all Jews, however sick. That night De Jong led NRK and ten other Jews out of the hospital and to his own home, where he hid and fed them for two years, until the American armies liberated Holland. When informed of a Nazi house-to-house hunt for Jews, he took his guests to another hideout until the raid was over, then brought them back home. If anyone fell sick, he would bring in a trusted doctor. He even got people to a dentist when they suffered from toothaches.

Johtje Vos and her husband Aart were part of the Dutch underground effort to save Jews. Although they had four small children, they risked their family's safety. Were they ever afraid? "Oh, God, yes!" said Mrs. Vos:

I was scared to death. And very near death also. At one point I was in the hands of the Gestapo, my husband

*was in jail, and the Nazis were doing a lot of house
searching. We were hiding 36 people, 32 Jews and four
others who were also being sought by the Gestapo. We
had made a tunnel underground from our house to a
nature reservation, and when we got a warning or had
an inkling that the village was surrounded, they all went
in there. They all came through because we had a house
in which we could do such things. It was not always easy
and often we were frightened, but we were able to help
a little bit, and we did it because we believed it was the
right thing to do.*

Long after the war, people still ask the Voses why they
helped Jews. Mrs. Vos answers:

*Well, my husband and I never sat down and discussed
it or said, "Let's go and help some Jews." It happened.
It was a spontaneous reaction, actually. Such things, such
responses depend on fate, on the result of your upbringing, your character, on your general love for people, and
most of all, on your love for God. And, I would say, there
was also a kind of nonchalance and optimism about it.
I would say to myself, "Oh come on, you can do that."*
*It also helped to have a happy marriage, because when
you feel strong at home . . . you can be strong for other
people.*

Sometimes it was the sight of Nazi brutality that aroused
Christians to act. Marion Pritchard, a Dutch student in
Nymegen, was bicycling past a small home for Jewish
children when she saw the Germans loading crying little
children on trucks. When they didn't move fast enough,

the Nazis grabbed them by an arm or a leg or the hair and threw them onto the trucks. Two women coming by tried to interfere, and the Nazis threw them in the truck, too. Marion couldn't believe men would treat babies this way. Crying with rage, she just sat there on her bicycle and at that moment decided she would do anything she could to stop such atrocities.

She joined with ten close friends who felt as she did to organize what aid they could for the Jews. They found hiding places and provided food, clothing and ration cards for the fugitives, and relief for the families concealing Jews. They registered newborn Jewish babies as Gentiles and got them medical care. When Marion learned of a father with three small children who needed refuge, she got an elderly friend of her parents' to let them all, herself included, move into her house in the country. There they all hid for the next two years, until the war's end. They built a secret place under the floor to hide in during Nazi raids.

Once four Germans with a Dutch Nazi policeman searched the house and found nothing. But knowing that it could pay to send someone back quickly, because Jews might be caught out of their hiding place, the police sent the Dutch Nazi back alone. The children had started to cry, so Marion had let them out. The policeman pushed his way in. She tells what happened:

I had a small revolver that a friend had given me, but I never planned to use it. I felt I had no choice except to kill him. I would do it again, under the same circumstances. But it still bothers me, and I still feel that there "should" have been another way. If anyone had really

140

tried to find out how and where he disappeared, they could have, but the general attitude was that there was one less traitor to worry about. A local undertaker helped dispose of the body; he put it in a coffin with a legitimate body in it. I hope that the dead man's family would have approved.

How many Jews survived in Holland? Perhaps 25,000 hid in the Christian world, but many thousands of them—the exact figure is unknown—were denounced and lost their lives. Out of 125,000 Jews about three quarters died. So despite the courage of good people, the Dutch were not able to save a large part of the Jews.

In Belgium rescue was more successful. Out of a Jewish population of 57,000 in 1940–1941, 29,000 survived—more than 50 percent. As in Denmark, the Jews were not seen as "good" or "bad" but simply as people in danger who must be helped for the sake of the community's and the individual's moral well-being. And the Belgian Jews moved quickly to help themselves; they were not passive in the face of extinction. They were aided by the Belgian underground, by the Socialists and Communists, and by leaders of the Catholic Church.

King Leopold and his mother, Queen Elizabeth, and various civil officials used their power and knowledge to get around Nazi edicts against the Jews. When the government went into exile in London, it declared it would not recognize any attempts to persecute the Jews or take away their property. Thus it let the Belgian people know it would denounce anyone trying to profit from the suffering of the Jews.

Belgians would not buy Jewish property stolen by the Nazis. The stock exchange refused to accept securities belonging to missing Jews. When the Nazis ordered Jews to wear yellow stars, Christians strolled the streets wearing the same star. In August 1942 the first group of Belgian Jews was deported to Auschwitz. The Belgian police sabotaged the Nazis' effort by losing or misplacing files on Jews and forging documents for them.

Thousands of Jews were hidden by various Belgian groups, and large sums of money were raised to pay for false documents and to aid Jews in hiding. Priests, helped by generous neighbors, merchants, and officials, did much to save children especially. They were encouraged by a powerful attack upon the Nazis by Cardinal van Roey. "It is forbidden to Catholics to collaborate in the formation of an oppressive government," he said. "It's obligatory for all Catholics to work against such a regime." Many Belgians listened to the cardinal. Railway workers let Jews escape from deportation trains, and postal workers opened and intercepted messages to the Nazis from informers. Nevertheless, by September 1944, when the country was liberated, 25,000 Belgian Jews had lost their lives in Auschwitz.

There are many stories of individual Belgians who made it possible for their Jewish neighbors to survive. In Namur, Abbé Joseph André took care of a houseful of Jewish children. He had the aid of his bishop, of the Jesuits, and of the Sisters of Charity. The city's officials slipped him the essential false documents. A child he saved, Jacques Weinberg, recalls Father André's care:

He used to sit up all night, napping in his chair. He would not think of undressing and going to bed. There was the constant fear of a raid. If someone knocked on the door, Father André was on his feet. In a minute he had the children fleeing through a camouflaged exit to the neighboring house, where a doctor lived. All the neighbors cooperated. Without their help Father André could not have accomplished so much. The butchers of Namur as well as the grocers and other merchants provided him with food and necessities for the children.

Furthermore, the priest was deeply concerned to preserve his foster children's Jewish heritage. He taught them about Judaism and never preached his own faith. At great risk he helped them celebrate Passover with a seder.

Another priest, Louis Celis, took the four children of deported parents into his home for three years. They went to church so as to throw off suspicion, but privately he taught them the Torah and heard their Hebrew prayers. When one of the children reached the age of thirteen, he arranged for his bar mitzvah.

Father Édouard Froidure was already running a camp for hundreds of children when the Nazis invaded Belgium. Jews brought their children to him for concealment. He took them in and gave them false names and birth certificates. He rescued some 300 that way without help from anyone else. The Nazis finally caught up with him and sent him to a German camp. He was liberated when the Allied armies captured it.

There are other Belgians who deserve mention: Jeanne Damman, a young Catholic woman in Brussels who became the principal of an underground school for Jewish children; and Jeanne de Mulienaere, a Catholic journalist who joined a resistance group that saved 3,000 Jewish children, placing them in monasteries and convents or in private homes.

Most people in the Low Countries cursed the Nazis silently. But these brave men and women were ready to sacrifice their lives to prevent the tragedies Hitler brought about.

LITHUANIA

● Kovno

Vilna ●

EAST
PRUSSIA

● Minsk

POLAND
UNDER
GERMAN
RULE

Warsaw
●

● Lodz

Plaszow
Cracow
●● ● Tarnopol
● ● ●
Auschwitz ● Lvov

SLOVAKIA

● Budapest

HUNGARY

RUMANIA

Bucharest ●

● Belgrade

SERBIA

11 *A Piece of Bread, a Bowl of Soup*

Even in Auschwitz some non-Jewish prisoners facing death did what they could to ease the suffering of Jews sharing their fate. Some who have written about the Holocaust assume that there could have been no moral order in the death camps. That *human* kinds of behavior were impossible in those places. In a closed world ruled by death, they say, the killing machine reduced men and women to animals, stripped of all dignity and decency. They assume that the victims, forced to endure monstrous things at the hands of others, turned into jackals preying on their fellow victims.

But the testimony left by survivors of the camps, or in which survivors are quoted, contradicts those glib assumptions. Terrence des Pres made a study of that vast literature that amply documents the fact that nobody survived without help from others. Though "life in the camps was savage," he says in his book *The Survivor*, "yet there was *also* a web of mutual aid and encouragement . . . some minimal fabric of care, some margin of giving and receiving . . . essential to life in extremity." The impulse to solidarity was not stifled. The prisoners faced a choice: help only yourself or help one another. And many, by innumerable small deeds of help and mutual care, showed that the Nazis could not extinguish in them all trace of human solidarity.

"FF"—Jewish—was twenty when she was sent to Auschwitz. This after fourteen months in Blizyn, a Nazi labor camp where she worked with the other Jewish prisoners making clothing for the Germans on the Russian front. She entered Auschwitz barefoot, ragged, starving, the only one of her family still alive. Now a number tattooed on her arm—A-15794—became her name.

She was put to work outside the camp, digging trenches with a shovel on the banks of the Vistula. It was backbreaking labor, and she soon got sick. Sores covered her body. One day she watched a group of political prisoners—Gentiles—pass by her at work. One of them, a boy of seventeen, looked familiar. Suddenly he broke from his line and ran to her. They recognized each other. He was Kazik Wonisowski, from her hometown, Mozowiecki. Their families had been friendly before their arrests. FF tells what this chance encounter in living hell meant to her:

The next day, Zosia, Kazik's sister, walked into our Block. I recognized her immediately. We fell into each other's arms. She told me she heard about me from her brother, from Kazik. She gave me her dress as a gift— such a precious possession! She worked in the kitchen, and Kazik worked in the warehouse where they kept the clothes of the Jews who were burned in the crematorium. They were both sent here as political prisoners. The dress Zosia gave me not only helped me stay alive from day to day, it saved me from death during the selektsyes. These selections went on all the time. You were condemned to death during the selektsye not only if you were sick, or couldn't endure the slave labor anymore, but also if they found a tick on you, a scab, a boil. My body was covered with sores. Especially the legs. Zosia also gave me a pair of stockings. I stood at the selection in Zosia's dress and stockings. The top part of my body was naked, but without boils. Luckily, I passed all the selektsyes.

Kazik came, bringing me pants and a piece of bread with butter. These were all such precious gifts. They were even more precious as symbols of human friendship. This was very important in staying alive and kept up my hope I would survive this ordeal.

She did survive, and came to live in America, where she recorded her story.

In Auschwitz Jews encountered another Gentile prisoner, Doctor Adelaide Hautval. The daughter of a French Protestant pastor, she was deeply religious. In 1934, at the age of twenty-eight, she had qualified as a doctor and begun to work in psychiatric clinics. In the spring of 1942 she had been imprisoned in France because she was traveling without a permit from Vichy to the Nazi-occupied zone to attend her sick mother. The Germans took her to a prison in Bourges, where many Jews were being held. She saw how brutally the Gestapo treated them and protested. The Germans said, "Because you defend them, you can share their fate." They made her stitch a yellow star on her clothes and wear a band with the words "Friend of Jews."

149

The Nazis kept her in prison until January 1943, when they shipped her to Auschwitz. She was tattooed with the number 31802, and placed in Block 10. She was the only Gentile among hundreds of Jewish women from France, Greece, Holland, and Belgium. The notorious Block 10 was where the Nazis, in the name of "medical science," conducted hideous experiments upon the doomed Jewish women.

As the only doctor assigned to their day-to-day care, Dr. Hautval did all she could to help them. Typhus erupted in the block when a new convoy of women brought in the disease. The Nazi policy was to send every person with the dreaded infection to the gas chamber. Doctor Hautval knew the only chance to prevent their immediate death was not to report the epidemic but to conceal it. She hid the sick women on the upper level of the bunks, and treated them with a mother's loving care. Prisoners remember that she used to say to them, "Here we are all condemned to death: let us behave like human beings as long as we are still alive."

The German physicians who staffed Auschwitz held SS officers' rank. Two of them, Doctor Agrad and Doctor Edward Wirths, ordered Doctor Hautval to help them in their medical experiments. From the beginning of his regime Hitler had secured the cooperation of German doctors who violated their Hippocratic oath to "do no harm." In 1934 they had begun to sterilize the "unfit," which meant "the inferior races who breed like vermin," as Hitler put it. Between December 1939 and August 1942 his doctors secretly killed fifty to sixty thousand Germans—children and adults—they considered "unfit Aryans." Lethal injections or gas chambers were used, in a prelude to Auschwitz. When the Vatican and some German bishops and cardinals condemned the "mercy killings" as "contrary to both natural and divine law," Hitler halted them. But almost at the same moment he began gassing vastly greater numbers in Poland's death camps.

What the SS doctors in Auschwitz wanted of Dr. Hautval was assistance in their experiments in "gynecological medicine," as they called it. They explained they were only trying to develop new ways to detect early signs of cancer in the uterus. No, she replied, I won't take part in such experiments. She realized they were ruthlessly using helpless Jewish women to carry out criminal acts directly counter to their obligations to heal the sick. No one has the right to play with the lives of other human beings, she said. Nor would she assist them in such tasks as administering anesthesia or performing sterilizations.

Angered by her stubborn refusals, Doctor Wirths asked whether she knew the difference between "these people"—the Jews—and her people. To which she answered, "I have indeed perceived people different from myself, and you are one of them." She stood guard over the welfare of the Jewish women, always their "angel in white," as they called her. She lived to see Auschwitz destroyed, and after the war testified in the trials involving the evil complicity of many in the German medical profession in carrying out Hitler's "Final Solution."

It is understandable that most of the reports on Auschwitz by former inmates of the camp concentrate on one aspect: the destruction of human beings. Again and again there is hunger, sickness, torture, pain, death. But the same reports reveal another side too: the human relationships that grew between many prisoners and even between some prisoners and their SS guards. Or between the various ethnic groups represented in the camps. The deeply anti-Semitic feelings of Polish, Russian, and Ukrainian prisoners made the life of Jews in the camps even worse. Yet some people in these groups developed warm friendships with Jews and understood the magnitude of the Jewish tragedy.

One example is Wolf Glicksman's story about the prisoner Joseph Cyrankiewicz, the future postwar prime minister of Poland. In Auschwitz Cyrankiewicz was made a block clerk. Wolf Glicksman, a Polish Jew meeting Cyrankiewicz on Wolf's first day there, was handed a sizeable piece of bread. "This was the highest expression of human feeling in the camp," said Glicksman. Help also came to him from another, and most unlikely, Christian prisoner, Jan Mosdorf. Mosdorf had led the anti-Semitic youth movement in Poland before the war. But in Auschwitz Mosdorf often risked his own life to carry letters from Glicksman to a relative in the women's camp of Birkenau, where Mosdorf was assigned to work. And he would bring back to Glicksman scraps of food and clothing sent by that relative.

Why? Who can explain this behavior? Cyrankiewicz said that no one really knows the full truth about Auschwitz. And Glicksman believes that "this is true. There were daily executions on the one hand, and there was play, song, and drink on the other hand. Ordinary camp inmates died from hunger and exhaustion while at work, but there was a group of prisoners who had plenty to eat. There was the low degradation of a man waiting impatiently for another to be shot or killed in order to inherit his shoes or clothes, and there were instances of sublime human conduct."

152

The sublime conduct of Lorenzo Perrone is what Primo Levi encountered in Auschwitz and has passed on to us. Perrone was an Italian bricklayer, officially not a prisoner, working as an anything-but-voluntary civilian in Auschwitz. Levi, twenty-four years old, a Jewish chemist from Turin, had been captured with other Italian partisans late in 1943 and held in a detention camp. Two months later, together with about 600 other Italian Jews, he was deported to Auschwitz. Within two days of their arrival, 500 of them were dead. Levi was "baptized" 174517 with the tattoo he would carry on his left arm the rest of his life. He was put to work by the Nazis in their synthetic rubber factory in Auschwitz.

Quickly he was reduced to the condition of "a hollow man," he wrote, "on the bottom":

A fortnight after my arrival I already had the prescribed hunger, that chronic hunger unknown to free men, which makes one dream at night, and settles in all the limbs of one's body. . . . On the back of my feet I already have those numb sores that will not heal. I push wagons, I work with a shovel, I turn rotten in the rain, I shiver in the wind: already my own body is no longer mine: my belly is swollen, my limbs emaciated, my face is thick in the morning, hollow in the evening; some of us have yellow skin, others gray. When we do not meet for a few days we hardly recognize each other.

One day Levi overheard two civilian bricklayers putting up a wall, speaking the dialect of his region of Italy. One of the men was Lorenzo Perrone. He came from a village about sixty miles from Turin. They began to talk, although for a civilian worker to talk to a prisoner was punishable by several months' imprisonment. For somebody to help a prisoner was rare because it was so dangerous. But Lorenzo was "a very exceptional man," born a Catholic, but not a believer. A friendship began:

Lorenzo brought me a piece of bread and the remainder of his ration every day for six months; he gave me a vest of his, full of patches; he wrote a postcard on my behalf to Italy and brought me the reply. For all this he neither asked nor accepted any reward, because he was good and simple and did not think that one did good for a reward.

All this should not sound little . . . however little sense there may be in trying to specify why I, rather than thousands of others, managed to survive the test. I believe that it was really due to Lorenzo that I am alive today; and not so much for his material aid, as for his having constantly reminded me by his presence, by his natural and plain manner of being good, that there still existed a just world outside our own, something and someone still pure and whole, not corrupt, not savage, extraneous to hatred and terror; something difficult to define, a remote possibility of good, but for which it was worth surviving.

After the liberation the two men met again, in Italy. Levi learned that Lorenzo had helped some other prisoners too. A Frenchman, a Pole, not only an Italian. He felt compelled to help "out of pure moral reasons," said Levi. In the last few days of Auschwitz, just before the Soviet troops arrived, Lorenzo had brought Levi a bowl of soup, and apologized because the soup was dirty. Levi didn't ask why, but later when they met again in Italy Lorenzo explained that he was carrying the soup bowl when a bombing raid caught him, and he fell into a bomb crater. An explosion tossed sand and dirt into the soup and broke one of his eardrums. But he hadn't told Levi of that, because he didn't want him to feel indebted.

"Lorenzo was a man," Levi concludes. "His humanity was pure and uncontaminated, he was outside this world of negation. Thanks to Lorenzo, I managed not to forget that I myself was a man."

Levi named his son Lorenzo.

12   *Whoever Saves a Single Soul*

We wonder why not much attention has been paid to the acts of Gentiles who risked their lives to rescue Jews during the Nazi era. One reason may be that against the immense darkness of the Holocaust, the light shone by the rescuers is only a tiny flicker. But we should not try to match the one against the other. Another reason may be a general cynicism about human goodness. Many believe that it is instinctive and natural for people to behave aggressively, to do harm to others. They think that when a good deed is done, it is only because the doer takes a selfish satisfaction in it. It gratifies his or her ego. They suspect the motives of gentle, friendly people who wish to love.

Or does the example of a rescuer make us worry about our own decency and compassion? When we read about an Eichmann we may feel sure we would never do anything so terrible. But when we read about an André Trocmé or a Raoul Wallenberg, we are challenged. Would I, could I, we wonder, stand up for the persecuted and the helpless? Would I risk so much? Would I care that much?

The answer lies partly in compassion and partly in

conscience. To feel compassion is to suffer with another. You are a bystander, you don't bear the same degree or kind of suffering. But you are able to enter imaginatively into the realm of another's pain. That fellowship of feeling, however, may not move you to action, may not prompt you to *do* something to lessen the other person's pain or to extricate that person from the situation causing the suffering.

What brings about action is often conscience. Conscience, we know, is our sense of right or wrong, of the moral goodness or blameworthiness of our own conduct or intention, together with the feeling that we are obliged to do or be what is regarded as good.

In the time of the Holocaust, it was this ability to respond to acts of evil—"response-ability" as des Pres calls it—that made attempts at rescue possible. The rescuers made a moral judgment about the evil deeds and events they confronted, and then they acted. They felt compassion for the suffering of others, and that compassion closed the distance between their own condition and that of another. And so they acted, bound in the oneness of humanity.

Of course rescue was never a simple thing. The historians of the "Final Solution" in the occupied countries discuss a great variety of circumstances that affected how far the mass murder went, and how far rescue succeeded. History, religion, class, politics, friendship, individualism—all were factors playing their part, and in the preceding chapters some of these have been touched upon.

Yehuda Bauer, the author of several studies of the Holocaust, concludes that "religious convictions had apparently less to do with attitudes to Jews than did national

157

backgrounds, historical traditions, or political views. On the whole, the tragic situation of the Jew in a Gentile environment was one in which the Jew could only appeal to feelings of mercy, compassion, and loving kindness. In some places he met people who had these qualities; in most places he did not."

In Israel there is a place where the deeds of the good people are recorded. It is called Yad Vashem—the Martyrs' and Heroes' Remembrance Authority. It is situated on a hilltop on the western edge of Jerusalem. It was established by the Israeli legislature in 1953 as a center for research on the Nazi Holocaust. It also contains a museum, a library, and archives.

An avenue of evergreen carob trees leads the visitor to the Holocaust Museum and the plaza dedicated to the heroism and martyrdom of the Warsaw Ghetto Uprising. It is called the Avenue of the Righteous. Each tree in it is planted to remember a Gentile who risked his or her life for Jews. By 1986 some 16,000 trees had been planted in the avenue and on a terraced hillside beyond the plaza. Many more cases await consideration by a special committee that studies the evidence for those who may qualify for the title "Righteous Gentile." When a case is confirmed, a tree is planted in that name, and a medal and certificate given to the person or a representative. On the medal is the inscription "Whoever saves a single soul, it is as if he had saved the whole world."

On each tree is a plaque with the name and nationality of the honored man or woman. The full story of each of them can be found in the archives of Yad Vashem. Many— in fact most of the men and women whose stories are told in this book—are honored at Yad Vashem.

They are, all of them, human spirits whose lives witness the truth that there *is* an alternative to the passive acceptance of evil. Where they lived, goodness happened. And where we live, goodness *can* happen.

Bibliography

The sources for this book are quite varied. They include autobiographies, biographies, memoirs, journals, diaries, oral histories, personal interviews, periodicals, letters, and historical studies of one or another aspect of the Holocaust that bear on my main interest. The reader who wants more information on the Holocaust itself has a huge literature to examine. In my earlier book *Never to Forget: The Jews of the Holocaust*, I offered an extensive list of titles, arranged by category of interest. The literature has grown considerably since then, of course.

I owe warmest thanks to a number of authors whose books were especially helpful: the late Philip Friedman for his pioneering survey of rescuers in Nazi-occupied Europe; John Bierman and Elenore Lester for their detailed portraits of Raoul Wallenberg; Philip Hallie for his thoughtful, loving, and inspiring portraits of the Trocmés and the villagers of Le Chambon; Thomas Keneally for his riveting story of the incredible Oskar Schindler; Nechama Tec for her scholarly investigation of the forces that prompted Christian rescue of Jews in Poland; Leonard Gross for his brilliantly orchestrated account of those who rescued Jews in Hitler's Berlin, and Susan Zuccotti for her careful study of Italy in the Holocaust.

160

Bauer, Yehuda. *Flight and Rescue: The Organized Escape of the Survivors of Eastern Europe, 1945–1948.* New York: Random House, 1970.

———. *A History of the Holocaust.* New York: F. Watts, 1982.

———. *The Holocaust in Historical Perspective.* Seattle: University of Washington Press, 1978.

Bierman, John. *Righteous Gentile: The Story of Raoul Wallenberg, Missing Hero of the Holocaust.* New York: Viking, 1981.

Chary, Frederick B. *The Bulgarian Jews and the Final Solution, 1940–1944.* Pittsburgh: University of Pittsburgh Press, 1972.

Dawidowicz, Lucy. *The Holocaust and History.* Cambridge, Mass.: Harvard University Press, 1981.

———. *The War Against the Jews, 1933–1945.* New York: Holt, Rinehart and Winston, 1975.

Des Pres, Terrence. *The Survivor: An Anatomy of Life in the Death Camps.* New York: Oxford University Press, 1976.

Epstein, Helen. *Children of the Holocaust: Conversations with Sons and Daughters of Survivors.* New York: Putnam, 1979.

Fogelman, F. and V. L. Wiener. "The Few, the Brave, the Noble." *Psychology Today* (August 1985): 60–65.

Frank, Anne. *The Diary of a Young Girl.* Translated from the Dutch by B. M. Mooyaart-Doubleday. Introduced by Eleanor Roosevelt. Garden City, N.Y.: Doubleday, 1967.

Friedlander, Saul. *When Memory Comes.* Translated from the French by Helen R. Lane. New York: Farrar Straus Giroux, 1979.

Friedman, Philip. *Their Brothers's Keepers: The Christian Heroes and Heroines Who Helped the Oppressed Escape the Nazi Terror.* New York: Crown Publishers, 1957.

Gies, Miep, with Alison Leslie Gold. *Anne Frank Remembered.* New York: Simon & Schuster, 1987.

Gilbert, Martin. *The Holocaust.* New York: Oxford University Press, 1986.

Glatstein, Jacob, ed. *Anthology of Holocaust Literature.* New York: Atheneum, 1972.

Gross, Leonard. *The Last Jews in Berlin.* New York: Simon and Schuster, 1982.

Gutman, Yisrael and Livia Rothkirchen, eds. *The Catastrophe of European Jewry: Antecedents, History, Reflections.* New York: KTAV, n.d.

Hallie, Philip. *Lest Innocent Blood Be Shed: The Story of the Village of Le Chambon and How Goodness Happened There.* New York: Harper & Row, 1979.

Hellman, Peter. *Avenue of the Righteous.* New York: Atheneum, 1980.

Henry, Frances. *Victims and Neighbors: A Small Town in Nazi Germany Remembered.* South Hadley, Mass.: Bergin & Harvey, 1984.

Huneke, Douglas D. *The Moses of Rovno: The Stirring Story of Fritz Graeve. . . .* New York: Dodd Mead, 1985.

Keneally, Thomas. *Schindler's List.* New York: Simon & Schuster, 1982.

Kren, George M. and Leon H. Rappoport. *The Holocaust and the Crisis of Human Behavior.* New York: Holmes & Meier, 1980.

Lester, Elenore. *Wallenberg: The Man in the Iron Web.* Englewood Cliffs, N.J.: Prentice-Hall, 1982.

Levi, Primo. *Moments of Reprieve*. Translated from the Italian by Ruth Feldman. New York: Summit, 1986.

———. *Survival in Auschwitz*. Translated from the Italian by Stuart Woolf. New York: Collier Books, 1971.

Levin, Nora. *The Holocaust: The Destruction of European Jewry, 1933–1945*. New York: Crowell, 1968.

Lukas, Richard C. *The Forgotten Holocaust: The Poles Under German Occupation, 1939–1944*. Lexington: University Press of Kentucky, 1986.

Macaulay, Jacqueline R. and Leonard Berkowitz, eds. *Altruism and Helping Behavior*. New York: Academia Press, 1970.

Marrus, Michael R. and Robert O. Paxton. *Vichy France and the Jews*. New York: Basic Books, 1981.

Mason, Henry L. "Jews in the Occupied Netherlands." *Political Science Quarterly* 99: 2 (Summer 1984).

Rabinowitz, Dorothy. *New Lives: Survivors of the Holocaust Living in America*. New York: Knopf, 1976.

Ramati, Alexander, as told by Padre Rufino Niccacci. *The Assisi Underground*. New York: Stein & Day, 1978.

Rittner, Carol and Sondra Myers, eds. *The Courage to Care: Rescuers of Jews During the Holocaust*. New York: New York University Press, 1986.

Tec, Nechama. *Dry Tears: The Story of a Lost Childhood*. New York: Oxford University Press, 1984.

———. *When Light Pierced the Darkness: Christian Rescue of Jews in Nazi-Occupied Poland*. New York: Oxford University Press, 1986.

Ten Boom, Corrie. *The Hiding Place*. New York: Bantam, 1974.

Trunk, Isaiah. *Jewish Responses to Nazi Persecution*. New York: Stein & Day, 1979.

Vago, Bela and George L. Mosse, eds. *Jews and Non-Jews in Eastern Europe, 1918–1945.* New York: Wiley, 1974.

Wyman, David S. *Abandonment of the Jews: America and the Holocaust, 1941–1945.* New York: Pantheon, 1984.

Yahil, Leni. *The Rescue of Danish Jewry: Test of a Democracy.* Translated from the Hebrew by Morris Gradel. Philadelphia: Jewish Publication Society 1983.

Zuccotti, Susan. *The Italians and the Holocaust: Persecution, Rescue, and Survival.* New York: Basic Books, 1987.

For those who seek additional resources, these books are recommended:

The Holocaust: An Annotated Bibliography and Resource Guide. Edited by David M. Szonyi. New York: KTAV, 1985. Lists resources on subjects related to learning about or teaching the Holocaust, as well as to programming and commemoration.

The Holocaust and Genocide: A Search for Conscience. 2 vols. 2nd ed. Edited by Richard Flaim, Edwin W. Reynolds, et al. New York: Anti-Defamation League of B'nai Brith, 1986. Curriculum guide and anthology on the Holocaust with units on rescue.

The Holocaust: Catalog of Publications and Audio-Visual Materials. Compiled by the staff of the ADL Center International Center for Holocaust Studies, 823 United Nations Plaza, NYC 10017. Lists more than 100 annotated and graded resources in ten subject areas, including a section on resistance and rescue.

The Holocaust in Books and Films: A Selected and Annotated List. Rev. ed. Edited by Judith H. Muffs and Dennis B. Klein. New York: Hippocrene Books, 1986. Lists over 400 resources, new and classic.

164

Index

167